THE PENGUIN BOOK OF PUZZLES

The Penguin Book of Puzzles

edited by

GARETH MOORE

PENGUIN BOOKS

PENGUIN BOOKS

UK | USA | Canada | Ireland | Australia
India | New Zealand | South Africa

Penguin Books is part of the Penguin Random House group of companies
whose addresses can be found at global.penguinrandomhouse.com

This collection first published 2017

006

Introduced and edited by Gareth Moore

The moral right of the author has been asserted

Set in 10.25/14 pt Plantin Std
Typeset by Jouve (UK), Milton Keynes
Printed in Great Britain by Clays Ltd, Elcograf S.p.A.

A CIP catalogue record for this book is available from the British Library

ISBN: 978–0–718–18862–7

www.greenpenguin.co.uk

MIX
Paper from
responsible sources
FSC
www.fsc.org   FSC® C018179

Penguin Random House is committed to a
sustainable future for our business, our readers
and our planet. This book is made from Forest
Stewardship Council® certified paper.

Contents

Introduction

Welcome to *The Penguin Book of Puzzles*! This jam-packed volume contains hundreds of puzzles that represent the best of both old and new puzzling.

What you *won't* find in this book is all the 'usual suspects' – there are no crosswords or sudoku, for example. There are countless examples of these available already, including in almost every newspaper on sale the very day you read this. What you'll find here instead is a huge range of material, all designed to confuse, perplex and – hopefully – delight you. So if you're looking for something brand new, or so old it's new all over again, then this is the book for you!

Early Puzzles

The first chapter features a range of puzzles that run from the earliest recorded periods of human history through to the Victorian era, including two puzzles old enough to predate the celebrated 'Riddle of the Sphinx'. The puzzles included in this chapter are in fact *all* riddles, and the selection here is chosen so that they remain solvable to modern readers. This has meant discarding many of the most ancient riddles, such as the Fishermen of Ios' challenge to Homer to identify what they describe: 'What we caught we threw away; what we could not catch we kept.' The solution to this is at the end of this introduction.

Some surviving early puzzles are in Latin – none of these are included here, although one of the most remarkable of these is the two-dimensional palindromic word square found in the ruins at Pompeii, as well as at the Roman villa in Cirencester and elsewhere:

```
R O T A S
O P E R A
T E N E T
A R E P O
S A T O R
```

The word square is considered palindromic because it remains the same when you read it backwards and upwards, as well as the more usual across and down. The exact Latin translation of 'Sator Arepo Tenet Opera Rotas' is not certain, but it is often taken to mean something along the lines of 'The farmer Arepo works a plough'.

The letters of this word square can also be rearranged so they spell 'PATER NOSTER', the Latin for 'Our Father', in a cross shape. Two 'A's and two 'O's remain, which it is said represent alpha and omega, the start and end of the Greek alphabet – but more specifically often used biblically as a reference to Jesus, 'the beginning and the end'. Whether this was part of the original intent of whoever created the word square is not known for sure, but it is quite probably a later invention from the early Christian period:

```
                P
                A
                T
              A E O
                R
    P A T E R N O S T E R
                O
              O S A
                T
                E
                R
```

Victorian and Edwardian Puzzles

Moving on, the second to fifth chapters of the book are compiled from early twentieth-century puzzle books, featuring many puzzles and riddles that will be both unfamiliar and challenging to a modern readership, as well as some that remain in current circulation. We start with mathematical puzzles, which were once far more popular with a mainstream audience than nowadays, before progressing to chapters on geometric puzzles, logical and lateral-thinking puzzles, and word puzzles.

These older puzzles are of their period, written with a certainty about the world that no longer exists, and they allow an occasional bending-of-the-rules that might now be considered a little unfair. They have been arranged into chapters as carefully as possible, and in particular for those in the 'logical and lateral thinking' chapter you should keep your wits about you as to alternative possible explanations – if you find a number puzzle in this chapter, for example, then it probably relies on a trick. Perhaps it requires you to think in terms of Roman numerals, or in terms of the spelling of a number, or to use some other clever method to make the seemingly mathematical impossible become possible.

Some of the puzzles have been lightly edited, never to change the meat of the actual puzzle but simply to remove any now-irrelevant asides, or sometimes to remove outdated attitudes or references to the world – and very occasionally to remove parts of a puzzle that would be unsolvable to a modern reader, such as reliances on outdated vocabulary or long forgotten units.

Modern Puzzles

Finally, the last chapter brings us right up to date with a selection of competition puzzles from the World Puzzle Federation's 'Grand Prix' puzzle competitions for 2016 and 2017. In this tournament, competitors from all over the world compete to discover who is the year's best puzzler, over a wide range of puzzles and across several rounds. Try these selected puzzles, all from the 'casual' rounds of the tournament, and see how you would get on against the world's puzzle elite.

Practicalities

Immediately following this Introduction are a few pages setting out how pre-decimal currency once worked, since a small number of the mathematical puzzles rely on knowledge of old British coinage. It is always clear when a puzzle requires this knowledge, and you can simply refer back to this section if necessary.

The following pages also include a summary of the imperial units you will encounter in this book, since on occasion it will be necessary to understand how many of one fit into another, or perhaps to understand what type of measurement a particular unit refers to.

It's also well worth pointing out that the authors of these earlier puzzles were not afraid of fractions, or non-integer numbers. This applies even to units not often divided in modern puzzles, such as days of the week or ages – so don't discount the possibility that someone might be 23¾ years old as too unlikely, since that might well be the answer!

Solutions

And the Fishermen of Ios' riddle to Homer? The solution is 'lice', or sometimes 'fleas'. It is claimed in one ancient text that Homer died of pique from not being able to solve it. Hopefully a similar fate will not befall you as you work your way through this book! After all, if you get really stuck you can always take a look at the solutions at the back – or ask someone else to take a look for you, and give you a hint.

Good luck – and have fun!

Dr Gareth Moore, July 2017

Notes on the Puzzles

The majority of the puzzles in this book are reproduced from early twentieth-century books, and therefore some refer to pre-decimal currency and imperial measurements. Here is a guide to help you with these puzzles.

Pre-decimal Currency

Name	Notation	Value
Farthing	¼ d.	One quarter of a penny
Half penny	½ d.	One half of a penny
Penny	1 d.	1/12 of a shilling
Two pence	2 d.	Two pence (1/6 of a shilling)
Three pence	3 d.	Three pence (1/4 of a shilling)
Four pence	4 d.	Four pence (1/3 of a shilling)
Six pence	6 d.	Six pence (1/2 of a shilling)
Shilling	1 s.	Twelve pence
Florin	2 s.	Two shillings
Half crown	2 s. 6 d.	Two shillings and six pence
Double florin	4 s.	Four shillings
Crown	5 s.	Five shillings
Half sovereign	10 s.	Ten shillings (half of one pound)
Sovereign	£1	Twenty shillings or one pound
Guinea	£1 1s.	Twenty-one shillings

Distances

Name	Notation	Value
Nautical mile	nmi.	6,076 feet, or 1.151 miles
Mile	mi.	5,280 feet, 1,760 yards, or 320 rods
Furlong	fur.	660 feet, 220 yards, or 1/8 mile
Rod	rd.	5.5 yards, or 16.5 feet
Fathom	fth.	6 feet, or 72 inches
Yard	yd.	3 feet, or 36 inches
Foot	ft. or '	12 inches, or 0.333 yards
Inch	in. or "	0.083 feet, or 0.028 yards
Square mile	sq mi, or mi^2	640 acres, or 102,400 square rods
Acre	acre	4,840 square yards, or 43,560 square feet
Square rod	sq rd, or rd^2	30.25 square yards, or 0.00625 acres
Square yard	sq yd, or yd^2	1,296 square inches, or 9 square feet
Square foot	sq ft, or ft^2	144 square inches, or 0.111 square yards
Square inch	sq in, or in^2	0.0069 square feet, or 0.00077 square yards

Weights

Name	Notation	Value
Grain	gr.	1/7000 pounds
Drachm	dr.	1/256 pounds
Ounce	oz.	1/16 pounds
Pound	lb.	16 ounces
Stone	st.	14 pounds
Quarter	qr. or qtr.	28 pounds
Hundredweight	cwt.	112 pounds
Ton	ton.	2240 pounds

Liquid Measures

Name	Notation	Value
Bushel	bu.	4 pecks
Peck	pk.	2 gallons
Gallon	gal.	4 quarts
Quart	qt.	2 pints
Pint	pt.	4 gills
Gill	gi.	5 fluid ounces
Fluid ounce	fl. oz.	8 fluid drams
Fluid dram	fl. dr.	60 minims
Minim	min.	1/60 of a fluid dram

PUZZLES

Chapter 1. Early Puzzles

This chapter contains a collection of riddles from throughout human history, covering a period of almost four thousand years right up until the Victorian age. In each case, if no further instructions are given, you should try to work out what each riddle is referring to, or in other words to answer the implied question, 'What am I?'

1. **A Sumerian Riddle (circa 18th century BC)**

    There is a house. The blind enter it and then come out seeing. What is that house?

2. **Cleobulus' 'Year Riddle' (circa 6th century BC)**

    'A father had twelve children, and these twelve children each had thirty white sons and thirty black daughters, who are immortal although some die every day.' Who are the father, children, and grandchildren in this riddle?

3. **The Riddle of the Sphinx (circa 5th century BC)**

    What is it that walks on four legs in the morning, two legs in the afternoon and three legs in the evening?

4. Symphosius (circa 4th – 5th century)

a)

More have I borne than one body ought. Three souls did I have, all of which I had within me: a pair departed, but the third nearly perished too.

b)

Unlike my mother, in semblance different from my father, of mingled race, a breed unfit for progeny, of others I am born, and none is born of me.

5. Aldhelm (circa 7th century)

a)

Long since, the holy power that made all things
So made me that my master's dangerous foes
I scatter. Bearing weapons in my jaws,
I soon decide fierce combats; yet I flee
Before the lashings of a little child.

b)

Six eyes are mine; as many ears have I;
Fingers and toes twice thirty do I bear.
Of these, when forty from my flesh are torn,
Lo, then but twenty will remain to me.

6. Claret (circa 14th century)

A vessel have I
That is round like a pear,
Moist in the middle,
Surrounded with hair;
And often it happens
That water flows there.

7. **Samuel Danforth (17th century)**

   The wooden birds are now in sight,

   Whose voices roar, whose wings are white,

   Whose mouths are fill'd with hose and shoes,

   With wine, cloth, sugar, salt and news,

   When they have eas'd their stomachs here

   They cry, farewell until next year.

8. **From *The Merry Book of Riddles* (17th century)**

   He went to the wood and caught it,

   He sat himself down and sought it;

   Because he could not find it,

   Home with him he brought it.

9. **Jonathan Swift (18th century)**

   From India's burning clime I'm brought,

   With cooling gales like zephyrs fraught.

   Not Iris, when she paints the sky,

   Can show more different hues than I;

   Nor can she change her form so fast,

   I'm now a sail, and now a mast.

   I here am red, and there am green,

   A beggar there and here a queen.

   I sometimes live in house of hair,

   And oft in hand of lady fair.

   I please the young, I grace the old,

   And am at once both hot and cold.

   Say what I am then, if you can,

   And find the rhyme, and you're the man.

10. **George Canning (18ᵗʰ century)**

    A word there is of plural number,

    Foe to ease and tranquil slumber;

    Any other word you take

    And add an *s* will plural make.

    But if you add an *s* to this,

    So strange the metamorphosis;

    Plural is plural now no more,

    And sweet what bitter was before.

11. **A Musician's Riddle (18ᵗʰ century)**

    From the mate of the cock, and winter-corn in the ground,

    The Christian name of my friend may be found:

    Join the song of a cat, to the place hermits dwell in,

    Gives the surname of him who does music excel in.

12. **Voltaire (18ᵗʰ century)**

    What of all things in the world is the longest, the shortest, the swiftest, the slowest, the most divisible and most extended, most regretted, most neglected, without which nothing can be done, and with which many do nothing, which destroys all that is little and ennobles all that is great?

13. **From Horatio Walpole's *Works* (18ᵗʰ century)**

    Before my birth I had a name,

    But soon as born I chang'd the same;

    And when I'm laid within the tomb,

    I shall my father's name assume.

    I change my name three days together

    Yet live but one in any weather.

14. From *The Penny Post* (18th century)

Take a word which is us'd to express a young lass.

A material which building contains.

A town you'll discover or I am an ass.

And you are a dunce for your pains.

15. From *The Gentleman and Lady's Town and Country Magazine* (18th century)

A thing whereon all Princes lie

And as we all express a sigh,

What man into the world brings in

An Indian weed whose leaf is thin;

A wood by Kings esteemed much

The part of speech when naming such:

These initials join'd declare

A town where friendly people are.

16. From *The Little Puzzling Cap* (18th century)

I have two eyes, both large and bright,

Tho' neither head, nor legs, nor feet,

A mouth too that will keenly bite,

Although I ne'er a morsel eat;

My meat my master makes his prey,

'Tis good against a rainy day.

17. Catherine Fanshawe (19th century)

'Twas in heaven pronounced – it was mutter'd in hell,*

And echo caught faintly the sound as it fell;

On the confines of earth 'twas permitted to rest,

And the depths of the ocean its presence confess'd.

'Twill be found in the sphere when 'tis riven asunder,

---

* This line was later edited by James Smith to create the more famous opening line of
' 'Twas whispered in Heaven, 'twas muttered in hell'.

Be seen in the lightning and heard in the thunder.

'Twas allotted to man with his earliest breath,

Attends at his birth and awaits him in death:

Presides o'er his happiness, honour, and health,

Is the prop of his house and the end of his wealth.

In the heaps of the miser 'tis hoarded with care,

But is sure to be lost on his prodigal heir.

It begins every hope, every wish it must bound,

With the husbandman toils, and with monarchs is crown'd.

Without it the soldier, the seaman may roam,

But woe to the wretch who expels it from home!

In the whispers of conscience its voice will be found,

Nor e'en in the whirlwind of passion is drown'd.

'Twill not soften the heart; and tho' deaf be the ear,

It will make it acutely and instantly hear.

Yet in shade let it rest like a delicate flower,

Ah, breathe on it softly – it dies in an hour.

18. From 'The Enigmas' column in *The Minerva* (19th century)

My first you will be,

If you're good and upright:

My second you'll see

In a sharp frosty night.

Together combined,

I'm a virtue that's great,

That should govern each mind,

And preside in each state.

19. **From *Farmer's Almanack* (19th century)**

Before creating Nature will'd
That atoms into form should jar,
By me the boundless space was fill'd
On me was hung the first-made star.
For me the saint will break his word;
By the proud atheist I'm rever'd;
At me the coward draws his sword,
And by the hero I am fear'd.
Scorned by the meek and humble mind,
Yet often by the vain possess'd,
Heard by the deaf, seen by the blind,
And to the troubled conscience rest.
Than Wisdom's sacred self I'm wiser,
And yet by every blockhead known;
I'm freely given by the miser,
Kept by the prodigal alone.
As vice deform'd, as virtue fair,
The courtier's loss, the patriot's gains.
The poet's purse, the coxcomb's care;
Read and you'll have me for your pains.

Chapter 2. Mathematical Puzzles

1. Concerning a Cheque

A man went into a bank to cash a cheque. In handing over the money the cashier, by mistake, gave him pounds for shillings and shillings for pounds. He pocketed the money without examining it, and spent half a crown on his way home, when he found that he possessed exactly twice the amount of the cheque. He had no money in his pocket before going to the bank, and it is an interesting puzzle to find out what was the exact amount of that cheque.

2. Pocket-money

I went down the street with a certain amount of money in my pocket, and when I returned home I discovered that I had spent just half of it, and that I now had just as many shillings as I previously had pounds, and half as many pounds as I then had shillings. How much money had I spent?

3. Dollars and Cents

An American correspondent tells me that a man went into a store and spent one-half of the money that was in his pocket. When he came out he found that he had just as many cents as he had dollars when he went in and half as many dollars as he had cents when he went in. How much money did he have on him when he entered?

4.   Loose Cash

What is the largest sum of money – all in current silver coins and no four-shilling-piece – that I could have in my pocket without being able to give change for half a sovereign?

5.   Doubling the Value

It is a curious fact that if you double £6 13s. you get £13 6s., which is merely changing the shillings and the pounds. Can you find another sum of money that has the same peculiarity that, when multiplied by any number you may choose to select, will merely exchange the shillings and the pounds? There is only one other multiplier and sum of money, beside the case shown, that will work. What is it?

6.   Generous Gifts

A generous man set aside a certain sum of money for equal distribution weekly to the needy of his acquaintance. One day he remarked, 'If there are five fewer applicants next week, you will each receive two shillings more.' Unfortunately, instead of there being fewer there were actually four more persons applying for the gift. 'This means,' he pointed out, 'that you will each receive one shilling less.' Now, how much did each person receive at that last distribution?

7.   Selling Eggs

A woman took a certain number of eggs to market and sold some of them. The next day, through the industry of her hens, the number left over had been doubled, and she sold the same number as the previous day. On the third day the new remainder was trebled, and she sold the same number as before. On the fourth day the remainder was quadrupled, and her sales the same as before. On the fifth day what had been left over were quintupled, yet she sold exactly the same as on all the previous occasions, and so disposed of her entire stock. What is the smallest number of eggs she could have taken to market the first day, and how many did she sell daily?

8.   Buying Buns

Buns were being sold at three prices: one a penny, two a penny, and three a penny. Some children (there were as many boys as girls) were given sevenpence to spend on these buns, each receiving exactly alike. How many buns did each receive? Of course no buns were divided.

9.   Unrewarded Labour

A man persuaded Weary Willie, with some difficulty, to try to work on a job for thirty days at eight shillings a day, on the condition that he would forfeit ten shillings a day for every day that he idled. At the end of the month neither owed the other anything, which entirely convinced Willie of the folly of labour. Now, can you tell just how many days' work he put in, and on how many days he idled?

10.   The Perplexed Banker

A man went into a bank with a thousand sovereigns and ten bags. He said, 'Place this money, please, in the bags in such a way that if I call and ask for a certain number of sovereigns you can hand me over one or more bags, giving me the exact amount called for without opening any of the bags.' How was it to be done? We are, of course, only concerned with a single application, but he may ask for any exact number of pounds from £1 to £1000.

11.   A Weird Game

Seven men engaged in play. Whenever a player won a game he doubled the money of each of the other players. That is, he gave each player just as much money as each had in his pocket. They played seven games and, strange to say, each won a game in turn in the order of their names, which began with the letters A, B, C, D, E, F and G. When they had finished it was found that each man had exactly two shillings and eightpence in his pocket. How much had each man in his pocket before play?

12. Find the Coins

Three men, Abel, Best and Crewe, possessed money, all in silver coins. Abel had one coin fewer than Best and one more than Crewe. Abel gave Best and Crewe as much money as they already had, then Best gave Abel and Crewe the same amount of money as they then held, and finally Crewe gave Abel and Best as much money as they then had. Each man then held exactly ten shillings. To find what amount each man started with is not difficult. But the sting of the puzzle is in the tail. Each man held exactly the *same coins* (the fewest possible) amounting to ten shillings. What were the coins and how were they originally distributed?

13. An Easy Settlement

Three men, Andrews, Baker and Carey, sat down to play at some game. When they put their money on the table it was found that they each possessed two coins only, making altogether £1 4s. 6d. At the end of play Andrews had lost five shillings and Carey had lost sixpence, and they all squared up by simply exchanging the coins. What were the exact coins that each held on rising from the table?

14. Digging a Ditch

Here is a curious question that is more perplexing than it looks at first sight. Abraham, an infirm old man, undertook to dig a ditch for two pounds. He engaged Benjamin, an able-bodied fellow, to assist him and share the money fairly according to their capacities. Abraham could dig as fast as Benjamin could shovel out the dirt, and Benjamin could dig four times as fast as Abraham could do the shovelling. How should they divide the money? Of course, we must assume their relative abilities for work to be the same in digging or shovelling.

15. Name their Wives

A man left a legacy of £1000 to three relatives and their wives. The wives received together £396. Jane received £10 more than Catherine, and Mary received £10 more than Jane. John Smith was given just as much as his wife, Henry Snooks got half as much again as his wife, and Tom Crowe received twice as much as his wife. What was the Christian name of each man's wife?

16. Market Transactions

A farmer goes to market and buys a hundred animals at a total cost of £100. The price of cows being £5 each, sheep £1 each, and rabbits 1s. each, how many of each kind does he buy? Most people will solve this, if they succeed at all, by more or less laborious trial, but there are several direct ways of getting the solution.

17. Their Ages

If you add the square of Tom's age to the age of Mary, the sum is 62; but if you add the square of Mary's age to the age of Tom, the result is 176. Can you say what are the ages of Tom and Mary?

18. Mrs Wilson's Family

Mrs Wilson had three children, Edgar, James, and John. Their combined ages were half of hers. Five years later, during which time Ethel was born, Mrs Wilson's age equalled the total of all her children's ages. Ten years more have now passed, Daisy appearing during that interval. At the latter event Edgar was as old as John and Ethel together. The combined ages of all the children are now double Mrs Wilson's age, which is, in fact, only equal to that of Edgar and James together. Edgar's age also equals that of the two daughters. Can you find all their ages?

19. De Morgan and Another

Augustus de Morgan, the mathematician, who died in 1871, used to boast that he was x years old in the year x^2. My living friend*, Jasper Jenkins, wishing to improve on this, tells me he was a^2+b^2 in a^4+b^4; that he was $2m$ in the year $2m^2$; and that he was $3n$ years old in the year $3n^4$. Can you give the years in which De Morgan and Jenkins were respectively born?

20. 'Simple' Arithmetic

When visiting a prison, I asked two inmates to give me their ages. They did so, and then, to test their arithmetical powers, I asked them to add the two ages together. One gave me 44 as the answer, and the other gave 1280. I immediately saw that the first had subtracted one age from the other, while the second person had multiplied them together. What were their ages?

* Note that 'living' here refers to the early 20ᵗʰ Century.

21.   A Dreamland Clock

In a dream, I was travelling in a country where they had strange ways of doing things. One little incident was fresh in my memory when I awakened. I saw a clock and announced the time as it appeared to be indicated, but my guide corrected me. He said, 'You are apparently not aware that the minute-hand always moves in the opposite direction to the hour-hand. Except for this improvement, our clocks are precisely the same as those you have been accustomed to.' Now, as the hands were exactly together between the hours of four and five o'clock, and they started together at noon, what was the real time?

22.   What is the Time?

At what time are the two hands of a clock so situated that, reckoning as minute points past XII, one is exactly the square of the distance of the other?

23.   Hill Climbing

Weary Willie went up a certain hill at the rate of one and a half miles per hour and came down at the rate of four and a half miles per hour, so that it took him just six hours to make the double journey. Now, how far was it to the top of the hill?

24.   Timing the Motor-car

'I was walking along the road at three and a half miles an hour,' said Mr Pipkins, 'when the motor-car dashed past me and only missed me by a few inches.'

'Do you know at what speed it was going?' asked his friend.

'Well, from the moment it passed me to its disappearance round a corner I took twenty-seven steps, and walking on reached that corner with one hundred and thirty-five steps more.'

'Then, assuming that you walked, and the car ran, each at a uniform rate, we can easily work out the speed.'

25. The Staircase Race

This is a rough sketch of the finish of a race up a staircase in which three men took part. Ackworth, who is leading, went up three risers at a time, as arranged; Barnden, the second man, went four risers at a time, and Croft, who is last, went five at a time.

Undoubtedly Ackworth wins. But the point is, how many risers are there in the stairs, counting the top landing as a riser?

I have only shown the top of the stairs. There may be scores, or hundreds, of risers below the line. It was not necessary to draw them, as I only wanted to show the finish. But it is possible to tell from the evidence the fewest possible risers in that staircase. Can you do it?

26. A Walking Puzzle

A man set out at noon to walk from Appleminster to Boneyham, and a friend of his started at two p.m. on the same day to walk from Boneyham to Appleminster. They met on the road at five minutes past four o'clock and each man reached his destination at exactly the same time. Can you say at what time they both arrived?

27.   Riding in the Wind

A man on a bicycle rode a mile in 3 minutes with the wind at his back, but it took him 4 minutes to return against the wind. How long would it take him to ride a mile if there was no wind?

Some will say that the average of 3 and 4 is 3½, and it would take him 3½ minutes. That answer is entirely wrong.

28.   A Rowing Puzzle

A crew can row a certain course upstream in 8 minutes, and, if there were no stream, they could row it in 7 minutes less than it takes them to drift down the stream. How long would it take to row down with the stream?

29.   The Moving Stairway

On one of the moving stairways on the London Tube I find that if I walk down twenty-six steps I require thirty seconds to get to the bottom, but if I make thirty-four steps I require only eighteen seconds to reach the bottom. What is the height of the stairway in steps? The time is measured from the moment the top step begins to descend to the time I step off the last step at the bottom on to the level platform.

30.   Sharing a Bicycle

Two brothers had to go on a journey and arrive at the same time. They had only a single bicycle, which they rode in turns, each rider leaving it in the hedge when he dismounted for the one walking behind to pick up, and walking ahead himself, to be again overtaken. What was their best way of arranging their distances? As their walking and riding speeds were the same, it is extremely easy. Simply divide the route into any *even* number of equal stages and drop the bicycle at every stage, using the cyclometer. Each man would then walk half-way and ride half-way.

But here is a case that will require a little more thought. Anderson and Brown have to go twenty miles and arrive at exactly the same time. They have only one bicycle. Anderson can only walk four miles an hour, while Brown can walk five miles an hour, but Anderson can ride ten miles an hour to Brown's eight miles an hour. How are they to arrange the journey? Each man always either walks or rides at the speeds mentioned, without any rests.

31. More Bicycling

Referring to the last puzzle, let us now consider the case where a third rider has to share the same bicycle. As a matter of fact, I understand that Anderson and Brown have taken a man named Carter into partnership, and the position today is this: Anderson, Brown and Carter walk respectively four, five and three miles per hour, and ride respectively ten, eight and twelve miles per hour. How are they to use that single bicycle so that all shall complete the twenty miles' journey at the same time?

32. A Side-car Problem

Atkins, Baldwin and Clarke had to go a journey of fifty-two miles across country. Atkins had a motor-bicycle with side-car for one passenger. How was he to take one of his companions a certain distance, drop him on the road to walk the remainder of the way, and return to pick up the second friend, who, starting at the same time, was already walking on the road, so that they should all arrive at their destination at exactly the same time? The motor-bicycle could do twenty miles an hour, Baldwin could walk five miles an hour, and Clarke could walk four miles an hour. Of course, each went at his proper speed throughout and there was no waiting. I might have complicated the problem by giving more passengers, but I have purposely made it easy, and all the distances are an exact number of miles – without fractions.

33. The Despatch-rider

If an army forty miles long advances forty miles while a despatch-rider gallops from the rear to the front, delivers a despatch to the commanding general, and returns to the rear, how far has he to travel?

34. The Two Trains

Two railway trains, one four hundred feet long and the other two hundred feet long, ran on parallel rails. It was found that when they went in opposite directions they passed each other in five seconds, but when they ran in the same direction the faster train would pass the other in fifteen seconds. Now, a curious passenger worked out from these facts the rate per hour at which each train ran. Can the reader discover the correct answer? Of course, each train ran with a uniform velocity.

35. Pickleminster to Quickville

Two trains, A and B, leave Pickleminster for Quickville at the same time as two trains, C and D, leave Quickville for Pickleminster. A passes C 120 miles from Pickleminster and D 140 miles from Pickleminster. B passes C 126 miles from Quickville and D half-way between Pickleminster and Quickville. Now, what is the distance from Pickleminster to Quickville? Every train runs uniformly at a sensible speed.

36. The Damaged Engine

We were going by train from Anglechester to Clinkerton, and an hour after starting some accident happened to the engine.

We had to continue the journey at three-fifths of the former speed, and it made us two hours late at Clinkerton, and the driver said that if only the accident had happened fifty miles farther on the train would have arrived forty minutes sooner. Can you tell from that statement just how far it is from Anglechester to Clinkerton?

37. The Puzzle of the Runners

Two men ran a race round a circular course, going in opposite directions. Brown was the best runner and gave Tompkins a start of one-eighth of the distance. But Brown, with a contempt for his opponent, took things too easily at the beginning, and when he had run one-sixth of his distance he met Tompkins, and saw that his chance of winning the race was very small. How much faster than he went before must Brown now run in order to tie with his competitor?

38. The Two Ships

Two ships sail from one port to another – two hundred nautical miles – and return. The *Mary Jane* travels outwards at twelve miles an hour and returns at eight miles an hour, thus taking forty-one and two-third hours for the double journey. The *Elizabeth Ann* travels both ways at ten miles an hour, taking forty hours on the double journey. Now, seeing that both ships travel at the average speed of ten miles per hour, why does the *Mary Jane* take longer than the *Elizabeth Ann?*

39. Find the Distance

A man named Jones set out to walk from A—— to B——, and on the road he met his friend Kenward, ten miles from A——, who had left B—— at exactly the same time. Jones executed his commission at B—— and, without delay, set out on his return journey, while Kenward as promptly returned from A—— to B——. They met twelve miles from B——. Of course, each walked at a uniform rate throughout. Now, how far is A—— from B——?

I will show the reader a simple rule by which the distance may be found by anyone in a few seconds without the use of a pencil. In fact, it is quite easy – when you know how to do it.

40. The Man and the Dog

'Yes; when I take my dog for a walk,' said a mathematical friend, 'he frequently supplies me with some interesting puzzle to solve. One day, for example, he waited, as I left the door, to see which way I should go, and when I started he raced along to the end of the road, immediately returning to me; again racing to the end of road and again returning. He did this four times in all, at a uniform speed, and then ran at my side the remaining distance, which according to my paces measured 27 yards. I afterwards measured the distance from my door to the end of the road and found it to be 625 feet. Now, if I walk 4 miles per hour, what is the speed of my dog when racing to and fro?'

41.　Baxter's Dog

This is an interesting companion to the 'Man and Dog' puzzle. Anderson set off from a hotel at San Remo at nine o'clock and had been walking an hour when Baxter went after him along the same road. Baxter's dog started at the same time as his master and ran uniformly forwards and backwards between him and Anderson until the two men were together. Anderson's speed is two, Baxter's four, and the dog's ten miles an hour. How far had the dog run when Baxter overtook Anderson? My correspondent in Italy who sends me this is an exact man, and he says, 'Neglect length of dog and time spent in turning.' I will merely add, neglect also the dog's name and the day of the month.

42.　Railway Shunting

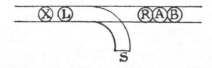

How are the two trains in our illustration to pass one another, and proceed with their engines in front? The small side-track is only large enough to hold one engine or one carriage at a time, and no tricks, such as ropes and flying-switches, are allowed. Every reversal – that is, change of direction – of an engine is counted as a move in the solution. What is the smallest number of moves necessary?

43.　Egg Laying

If a hen and a half lays an egg and a half in a day and a half, how many and a half who lay better by half will lay half a score and a half in a week and a half?

44.   The Flocks of Sheep

Four brothers were comparing the number of sheep that they owned. It was found that Claude had ten more sheep than Dan. If Claude gave a quarter of his sheep to Ben, then Claude and Adam would together have the same number as Ben and Dan together. If, then, Adam gave one-third to Ben, and Ben gave a quarter of what he then held to Claude, who then passed on a fifth of his holding to Dan, and Ben then divided one-quarter of the number he then possessed equally amongst Adam, Claude and Dan, they would all have an equal number of sheep. How many sheep did each brother possess?

45.   Pussy and the Mouse

'There's a mouse in one of these barrels,' said the dog.

'Which barrel?' asked the cat.

'Why, the five-hundredth barrel.'

'What do you mean by the five-hundredth? There are only five barrels in all.'

'It's the five-hundredth if you count backwards and forwards in this way.'

And the dog explained that you count like this:

1	2	3	4	5
9	8	7	6	
	10	11	12	13

So that the seventh barrel would be the one marked 3 and the twelfth barrel the one numbered 4.

'That will take some time,' said the cat, and she began a laborious count. Several times she made a slip, and had to begin again.

'Rats!' exclaimed the dog. 'Hurry up or you will be too late!'

'Confound you! You've put me out again, and I must make a fresh start.'

Meanwhile the mouse, overhearing the conversation, was working madly at enlarging a hole, and just succeeded in escaping as the cat leapt into the correct barrel.

'I knew you would lose it,' said the dog. 'Your education has been sadly neglected. A certain amount of arithmetic is necessary to every cat, as it is to every dog. Bless me! Even some snakes are adders!'

Now, which was the five-hundredth barrel? Can you find a quick way of arriving at the answer without making the actual count?

46.   Army Figures

A certain division in an army was composed of a little over twenty thousand men, made up of five brigades. It was known that one-third of the first brigade, two-sevenths of the second brigade, seven-twelfths of the third, nine-thirteenths of the fourth, and fifteen-twenty-seconds of the fifth brigade happened in every case to be the same number of men. Can you discover how many men there were in every brigade?

47.   A Critical Vote

A meeting of the Amalgamated Society of Itinerant Askers (better known as the 'Tramps' Union') was held to decide whether the members should strike for reduced hours and larger donations. It was arranged that during the count those in favour of the motion should remain standing, and those who voted against should sit down.

'Gentlemen,' said the chairman in due course, 'I have the pleasure to announce that the motion is carried by a majority equal to exactly a quarter of the opposition.' (Loud cheers.)

'Excuse me, guv'nor,' shouted a man at the back, 'but some of us over here couldn't sit down.'

'Why not?'

' 'Cause there ain't enough chairs.'

'Then perhaps those who wanted to sit down but couldn't will hold up their hands . . . I find there are a dozen of you, so the motion is lost by a majority of one.' (Hisses and disorder.)

Now, how many members voted at that meeting?

48.   The House Number

A man said the house of his friend was in a long street, numbered on his side one, two, three, and so on, and that all the numbers on one side of him added up to exactly the same as all the numbers on the other side of him. He said he knew there were more than fifty houses on that side of the street, but not so many as five hundred.

Can you discover the number of that house?

49.   Another Street Puzzle

A long street in Brussels has all the odd numbers of the houses on one side and all the even numbers on the other – a method of street numbering quite common in our own country. (1) If a man lives in an odd-numbered house and all the numbers on one side of him, added together, equal the numbers on the other side, how many houses are there, and what is the number of his house? (2) If a man lives on the even side and all the numbers on one side of him equal those on the other side, how many houses are there, and what is his number? We will assume that there are more than fifty houses on each side of the street and fewer than five hundred.

50.   Correcting an Error

Hilda Wilson was given a certain number to multiply by 409, but she made a blunder that is very common with children when learning the elements of simple arithmetic: she placed the first figure of her product by 4 below the second figure from the right instead of below the third. We have all done that as youngsters when there has happened to be a 0 in the multiplier. The result of Hilda's mistake was that her answer was wrong by 328,320, entirely in consequence of that little slip. Now, what was the multiplicand – the number she was given to multiply by 409?

51.   Adding their Cubes

The numbers 407 and 370 have this peculiarity, that they exactly equal the sum of the cubes of their digits. Thus the cube of 4 is 64, the cube of 0 is 0, and the cube of 7 is 343. Add together 64, 0, and 343, and you get 407. Again, the cube of 3 (27), added to the cube of 7 (343), is 370. Can you find a number not containing a nought that will work in the same way? Of course, we bar the absurd case of 1.

52.   Squares and Cubes

Can you find two whole numbers, such that the difference of their squares is a cube and the difference of their cubes is a square? What is the answer in the smallest possible numbers?

53.   A Common Divisor

Find a common divisor for the three numbers, 480,608, 508,811 and 723,217, so that the remainder shall be the same in every case.

54. The Rejected Gun

An inventor offered a new large gun to the committee appointed by our Government for the consideration of such things. He declared that when once loaded it would fire sixty shots at the rate of a shot a minute. The War Office put it to the test and found that it fired sixty shots an hour, but declined it, 'as it did not fulfil the promised condition.' 'Absurd,' said the inventor, 'for you have shown that it clearly does all that we undertook it should do.' 'Nothing of the sort,' said the experts. 'It has failed.' Now, can you explain this extraordinary mystery? Was the inventor, or were the experts, right?

55. Odds and Evens

Here is a little parlour trick, the explanation of which is quite easy. Ask a friend to take an even number of coins in one hand and an odd number in the other. You then undertake to tell him which hand holds the odd and which the even. Tell him to multiply the number in the right hand by 7 and the number in the left by 6, add the two products together, and tell you the result. You can then immediately give him the required answer. How are you to do it?

56. The Nine Barrels

In how many different ways may these nine barrels be arranged in three tiers of three so that no barrel shall have a smaller number than its own below it or to the right of it? The first correct arrangement that will occur to you is 1 2 3 at the top, then 4 5 6 in the second row, and 7 8 9 at the bottom, and my sketch gives a second arrangement. How many are there altogether?

57.   A Picture Presentation

A wealthy collector had ten valuable pictures. He proposed to make a presentation to a public gallery, but could not make up his mind as to how many he would give. So it amused him to work out the exact number of different ways. You see, he could give any one picture, any two, any three, and so on, or give the whole ten. The reader may think it a long and troublesome calculation, but I will give a little rule that will enable him to get the answer in all such cases without any difficulty and only trivial labour.

58.   A General Election

In how many different ways may a Parliament of 615 members be elected if there are only four parties: Conservatives, Liberals, Socialists and Independents? You see you might have C. 310, L. 152, S. 150, I. 3; or C. 0, L. 0, S. 0, I. 615; or C. 205, L. 205, S. 205, I. 0; and so on. The candidates are indistinguishable, as we are only concerned with the party numbers.

59.   The Magisterial Bench

A bench of magistrates consists of two Englishmen, two Scotsmen, two Welshmen, one Frenchman, one Italian, one Spaniard and one American. The Englishmen will not sit beside one another, the Scotsmen will not sit beside one another, and the Welshmen also object to sitting together. Now, in how many different ways may the ten men sit in a straight line so that no two men of the same nationality shall ever be next to one another?

60. The Card Pentagon

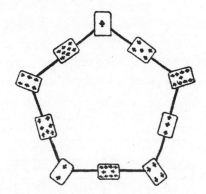

Make a rough pentagon on a large sheet of paper. Then throw down the ten non-court cards of a suit at the places indicated in the illustration, so that the pips on every row of three cards on the sides of the pentagon shall add up alike. The example will be found faulty. After you have found the rule you will be able to deal the cards into their places without any thought. And there are very few ways of placing them.

61. A Heptagon Puzzle

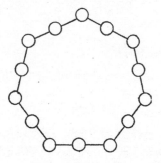

Using the fourteen numbers, 1, 2, 3, up to 14, place a different number in every circle so that the three numbers in every one of the seven sides add up to 19.

62. An Irregular Magic Square

Here we have a perfect magic square composed of the numbers 1 to 16 inclusive. The rows, columns, and two long diagonals all add up to 34. Now, supposing you were forbidden to use the two numbers 2 and 15, but allowed, in their place, to repeat any two numbers already used, how would you construct your square so that rows, columns, and diagonals should still add up to 34? Your success will depend on which two numbers you select as substitutes for the 2 and 15.

1	14	7	12
15	4	9	6
10	5	16	3
8	11	2	13

63. A Magic Square Delusion

Here is a magic square of the fifth order. Try to form such a magic square with 1 in the central cell.

17	24	1	8	15
23	5	7	14	16
4	6	13	20	22
10	12	19	21	3
11	18	25	2	9

64. Difference Squares

Can you rearrange the nine digits in the square so that in all the eight directions the difference between one of the digits and the sum of the remaining two shall always be the same? In the example shown it will be found that all the rows and columns give the difference 3; (thus 4+2–3, and 1+9–7, and 6+5–8, etc.), but the two diagonals are wrong, because 8–(4+1) and 6–(1+2) is not allowed: the sum of two must not be taken from the single digit, but the single digit from the sum. How many solutions are there?

4	3	2
7	1	9
6	5	8

65.   **Is it Very Easy?**

Here is a simple magic square, the three columns, three rows, and two diagonals adding up to 72. The puzzle is to convert it into a multiplying magic square, in which the numbers in all the eight lines if *multiplied* together give the same product in every case. You are not allowed to change, or add to, any of the figures in a cell or use any arithmetical sign whatever! But you may shift the two figures within a cell. Thus, you may write 27 as 72, if you like.

27	20	25
22	24	26
23	28	21

66.   **The Five-pointed Star**

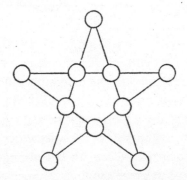

There is something very fascinating about star puzzles. I give an example, taking the case of the simple five-pointed star. It is required to place a different number in every circle so that the four circles in a line shall add up to 24 in all the five directions. No solution is possible with ten consecutive numbers, but you can use any whole numbers you like.

67.　The Six-pointed Star

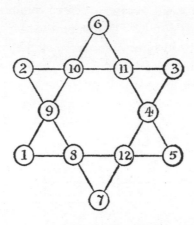

We have considered the question of the five-pointed star. We shall now find the six-pointed star even more interesting. In this case we can always use the twelve consecutive numbers 1 to 12 and the sum of the four numbers in every line will always be 26. The numbers at the six points of the star may add up to any even number from 24 to 54 inclusive, except 28 and 50, which are impossible. It will be seen that in the example I have given the six points add up to 24. If for every number in its present position you substitute its difference from 13 you will get another solution, its complementary, with the points adding up to 54, which is 78 less 24. The two complementary totals will always sum to 78. I will give the total number of different solutions and point out some of the pretty laws which govern the problem, but I will leave the reader this puzzle to solve. There are six arrangements, and six only, in which all the lines of four and the six points also add up to 26. Can you find one or all of them?

68. The Seven-pointed Star

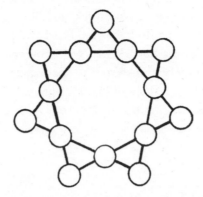

We have already dealt briefly with stars of five and six points. The case of the seven-pointed star is particularly interesting. All you have to do is to place the numbers 1, 2, 3, up to 14 in the fourteen discs so that every line of four discs shall add up to 30. If you make a rough diagram and use numbered counters, you will soon find it difficult to break away from the fascination of the thing. Possibly, however, not a single reader will hit upon a simple method of solution; his answer, when found, will be obtained by mere patience and luck. Yet, like those of the large majority of the puzzles given in these pages, the solution is subject to law, if you can unravel it.

69. Two Eight-pointed Stars

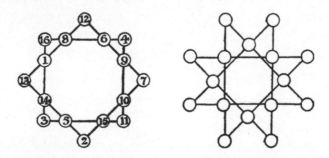

The puzzles of stars with five, six and seven points that I have given lead us to the eight-pointed star. The star may be formed in two different ways, as shown in our illustration, and the first example is a solution. The numbers 1 to 16 are so placed that every straight line of four adds up to 34. If you substitute for every number its difference from 17 you will get the complementary solution. Let the reader try to discover some of the other solutions, and he will find it a very hard nut, even with this one to help him. But I will present the puzzle in an easy and entertaining form. When you know how, every arrangement in the first star can be transferred to the second one automatically. Every line of four numbers in the one case will appear in the other, only the *order* of the numbers will have to be changed. Now, with this information given, it is not a difficult puzzle to find a solution for the second star.

70. The Damaged Measure

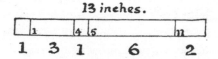

A man has a yard-stick from which 3 inches have been broken off, so that it is only 33 inches in length. Some of the graduation marks are also obliterated, so that only eight of these marks are legible; yet he is able to measure any given number of inches from 1 inch up to 33 inches. Where are these marks placed?

As an example, I give in the illustration the case of a 13-inch rod with four markings. If I want to measure 4 inches, I take 1 and 3; for 8 inches, 6 and 2; for 10 inches, 3, 1 and 6; and so on. Of course, the exact measure must be taken at once on the rod; otherwise the single mark of 1 inch repeated a sufficient number of times would measure any length, which would make the puzzle absurd!

71. The Six Cottages

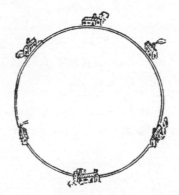

A circular road, twenty-seven miles long, surrounds a tract of wild and desolate country, and on this road are six cottages so placed that one cottage or another is at a distance of one, two, three up to twenty-six miles inclusive from some other cottage.

Thus, Brown may be a mile from Stiggins, Jones two miles from Rogers, Wilson three miles from Jones, and so on. Of course, they can walk in either direction as required. Can you place the cottages at distances that will fulfil these conditions? The illustration is intended to give no clue as to the relative distances.

72. A New Domino Puzzle

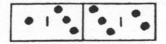

It will be seen that I have selected and placed together two dominoes so that by taking the pips in unbroken conjunction I can get all the numbers from 1 to 9 inclusive. Thus, 1, 2 and 3 can be taken alone; then 1 and 3 make 4; 3 and 2 make 5; 3 and 3 make 6; 1, 3 and 3 make 7; 3, 3 and 2 make 8; and 1, 3, 3 and 2 make 9. It would not have been allowed to take the 1 and the 2 to make 3, nor to take the first 3 and the 2 to make 5. The numbers would not have been in conjunction. Now try to arrange four dominoes so that you can make the pips in this way sum to any number from 1 to 23 inclusive. The dominoes need not be placed 1 against 1, 2 against 2, and so on, as in play.

73. At the Brook

A man goes to a brook with two measures of 15 pints and 16 pints. How is he to measure exactly 8 pints of water, in the fewest possible transactions? Filling or emptying a vessel or pouring any quantity from one vessel to another counts as a transaction. I need hardly add that no tricks, such as marking or tilting the vessels, are allowed.

74. A Prohibition Poser

The American Prohibition authorities discovered a full barrel of beer, and were about to destroy the liquor by letting it run down a drain when the owner pointed to two vessels standing by and begged to be allowed to retain in them a small quantity for the immediate consumption of his household. One vessel was a 7-quart and the other a 5-quart measure. The officer was a wag, and, believing it to be impossible, said that if the man could measure an exact quart into each vessel (without any pouring back into the barrel) he might do so. How was it to be done in the fewest possible transactions without any marking or other tricks? An American barrel of beer contains exactly 120 quarts.

75. Prohibition again

Let us now try to discover the fewest possible manipulations under the same conditions as in the last puzzle, except that we may now pour back into the barrel.

76.   The False Scales

A pudding, when put into one of the pans of these scales, appeared to weigh four ounces more than nine-elevenths of its true weight, but when put into the other pan it appeared to weigh three pounds more than in the first pan. What was its true weight?

77.   Weighing the Goods

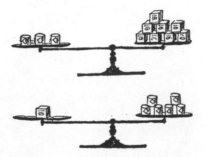

A tradesman whose morals had become corrupted during the war by a course of profiteering went to the length of introducing a pair of false scales. It will be seen from the illustration that one arm is longer than the other, though they are purposely so drawn as to give no clue to the answer. As a consequence, it happened that in one of the cases exhibited eight of the little packets (it does not matter what they contain) exactly balanced three of the canisters, while in the other case one packet appeared to be of the same weight as six canisters. Now, as the true weight of one canister was known to be exactly one ounce, what was the true weight of the eight packets?

78. Monkey and Pulley

A rope is passed over a pulley. It has a weight at one end and a monkey at the other. There is the same length of rope on either side and equilibrium is maintained. The rope weighs four ounces per foot. The age of the monkey and the age of the monkey's mother together total four years. The weight of the monkey is as many pounds as the monkey's mother is years old. The monkey's mother is twice as old as the monkey was when the monkey's mother was half as old as the monkey will be when the monkey is three times as old as the monkey's mother was when the monkey's mother was three times as old as the monkey. The weight of the rope and the weight at the end was half as much again as the difference in weight between the weight of the weight and the weight and the weight of the monkey. Now, what was the length of the rope?

79. Weighing the Baby

'I saw a funny incident at the railway station last summer,' said a friend. 'There was a little family group in front of the automatic weighing machine, that registered up to 200 lb., and they were engaged in the apparently difficult task of weighing the baby. Whenever they attempted to put the baby alone on the machine she always yelled and rolled off, while the father was holding off the dog, who always insisted on being included in the operations. At last the man, with the baby and Fido, were on the machine together, and I took this snapshot of them with my camera.'

He produced a photograph, from which I have simply copied the dial, as that is all we need.

'Then the man turned to his wife and said, 'It seems to me, my dear, that baby and I together weigh 162 lb. more than the dog, while the dog weighs 70 per cent less than the baby. We must try to work it out at home.' I also amused myself by working it out from those figures. What do you suppose was the actual weight of that dear infant?'

80. Packing Cigarettes

A manufacturer sends out his cigarettes in boxes of 160; they are packed in eight rows of twenty each, and exactly fill the box. Could he, by packing differently, get more cigarettes than 160 into the box? If so, what is the greatest number that he could add? At first sight it sounds absurd to expect to get more cigarettes into a box that is already exactly filled, but a moment's consideration should give you the key to the paradox.

81. Fallacious Reasoning

I prove 2 = 1, thus:

$x = a$; then:

$x^2 = ax$

$x^2 - a^2 = ax - a^2$

$(x + a)(x - a) = a(x - a)$

$x + a = a$

$2a = a$ (since $x = a$)

$2 = 1$

Who will detect the fallacy?

82. The Sheep

One man said to another, 'Give me one of your sheep, and I shall have twice as many as you.' The other replied, 'No, give me one of yours, and I shall have as many as you.' How many had each?

83.   Careful Division

Divide 45 in four parts, so that the first part with two added, the second with two subtracted, the third divided by two, the fourth multiplied by two, shall equal each other.

Chapter 3. Geometrical Puzzles

1. The Square Table-top

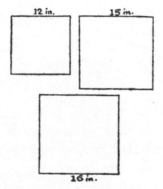

A man had three pieces of beautiful wood, measuring 12 in., 15 in., and 16 in. square respectively. He wanted to cut these into the fewest pieces possible that would fit together and form a small square tabletop 25 in. by 25 in. How was he to do it? I have found several easy solutions in six pieces, very pretty, but have failed to do it in five pieces. Perhaps the latter is not possible. I know it will interest my readers to examine the question.

2. A New Cutting-out Puzzle

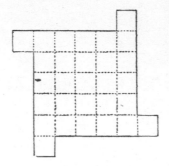

Cut the figure into four pieces that will fit together and form a square.

3. The Squares of Veneer

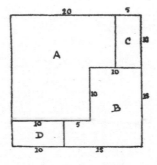

A man has two square pieces of valuable veneer, each measuring 25 in. by 25 in. One piece he cut, in the manner shown in our illustration, in four parts that will form two squares, one 20 in. by 20 in. and the other 15 in. by 15 in. Simply join C to A and D to B. How is he to cut the other square into four pieces that will form again two other squares with sides in exact inches, but not 20 and 15 as before?

4.   Dissecting the Moon

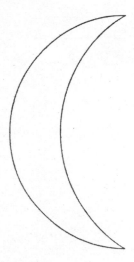

In how large a number of pieces can this crescent moon be cut with five straight cuts of the knife? The pieces may not be piled or shifted after a cut.

5.   Dissecting the Letter E

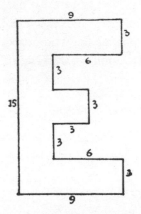

Can you cut this letter E into only five pieces so that they will fit together to form a perfect square? I have given all the measurements in inches so that there should be no doubt as to the correct proportions of the letter. In this case you are not allowed to turn over any piece.

6. Hexagon to Square

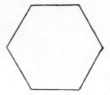

Can you cut this perfect hexagon into five pieces that will fit together and form a square?

7. Squaring a Star

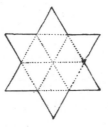

This six-pointed star can be cut into as few as five pieces that will fit together and form a perfect square. To perform the feat in seven pieces is quite easy, but to do it in five is more difficult. I introduce the dotted lines merely to show the true proportions of the star, which is thus built up of twelve equilateral triangles.

8. The Mutilated Cross

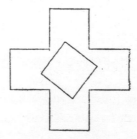

Here is a symmetrical Greek Cross from which has been cut a square piece exactly equal to one of the arms of the cross. The puzzle is to cut what remains into four pieces that will fit together and form a square. This is a pleasing but particularly easy cutting-out puzzle.

9.   The Victoria Cross

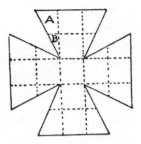

Cut the cross shown into seven pieces that will fit together and form a perfect square. Of course, there must be no trickery or waste of material.

In order that the reader may have no doubt as to the exact proportions of the cross as given, I have inserted the dotted lines. As the pieces A and B will fit together to form one of those little squares, it is clear that the area of the cross is equal to seventeen such squares.

10.   The Maltese Cross

Can you cut the star into four pieces and place them inside the frame so as to show a perfect Maltese Cross?

11.   The Pirates' Flag

Here is a flag taken from a band of pirates on the high seas. The twelve stripes represented the number of men in the band, and when a new man was admitted or dropped out a new stripe was added or one removed, as the case might be. Can you discover how the flag should be cut into as few pieces as possible so that they may be put together again and show only ten stripes? No part of the material may be wasted, and the flag must retain its oblong shape.

12.   The Crescent and the Star

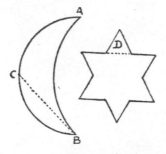

Here is a little puzzle on the Crescent and the Star. Look at the illustration, and see if you can determine which is the larger, the Crescent or the Star. If both were cut out of a sheet of solid gold, which would be the more valuable? As it is very difficult to guess by the eye, I will state that the outer arc, A C B, is a semicircle; the radius of the inner arc is equal to the straight line B C; the distance in a straight line from A to B is twelve inches; and the point of the star, D, contains three square inches. Now it is quite easy to settle the matter at a glance – when you know how.

13. The Patchwork Quilt

Here is a patchwork quilt that was produced by two young ladies for some charitable purpose. When they came to join their work it was found that each lady had contributed a portion of exactly the same size and shape. It is an amusing puzzle to discover just where these two portions are joined together. Can you divide the quilt into two parts, simply by cutting the stitches, so that the portions shall be of the same size and shape? You may think you have solved it in a few minutes, but – wait and see!

14. The Improvised Draughts-board

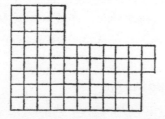

Some Englishmen at the front during the Great War wished to pass a restful hour at a game of draughts. They had coins and small stones for the men, but no board. However, one of them found a piece of linoleum as shown in the illustration, and, as it contained the right number of squares, it was decided to cut it and fit the pieces together to form a board, blacking some of the squares afterwards for convenience in playing. An ingenious Scotsman showed how this could be done by cutting the stuff in two pieces only, and it is a really good puzzle to discover how he did it. Cut the linoleum along the lines into two pieces that will fit together and form the board, eight by eight.

15.   Tessellated Pavements

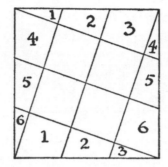

The reader must often have noticed, in looking at tessellated pavements and elsewhere, that a square space had sometimes to be covered with square tiles under such conditions that a certain number of the tiles have to be cut in two parts. A familiar example is shown in our illustration, where a square has been formed with ten square tiles. As ten is not a square number a certain number of tiles must be cut. In this case it is six. It will be seen that the pieces 1 and 1 are cut from one tile, 2 and 2 from another, and so on.

Now, if you had to cover a square space with exactly twenty-nine square tiles of equal size, how would you do it? What is the smallest number of tiles that you need cut in two parts?

16.   The Ribbon Pentagon

The solution to the following will be found very interesting if the reader has not seen it before. I want to form a regular pentagon, but the only thing at hand happens to be a rectangular strip of paper. How am I to do it without pencil, compasses, scissors, or anything else whatever but my fingers?

17. Paper Folding

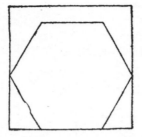

This is a branch of puzzledom both instructive and interesting. I do not refer to folding paper into the forms of boxes, boats, frogs and such things, but to the solving of certain geometrical problems with paper and fingers alone. I will give a comparatively easy example. Suppose you are given a perfectly square piece of paper, how are you going to fold it so as to indicate by creases a regular hexagon, as shown in the illustration, all ready to be cut out? Of course, you must use no pencil, measure, or instrument of any kind whatever. The hexagon may be in any position in the square.

18. Folding a Pentagon

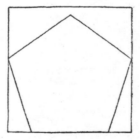

Here is another puzzle in paper folding of a rather more difficult character than the hexagon example that we have considered. If you are given a perfectly square piece of paper, how are you to fold it so as to indicate by creases a regular pentagon, as in our illustration, all ready to be cut out? Remember that you must use your fingers alone, without any instrument or measure whatever.

19. Making an Octagon

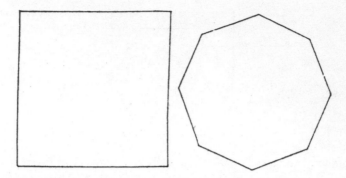

Can you cut the regular octagon from a square piece of paper without using compasses or ruler, or anything but scissors? You can fold the paper so as to make creases.

20. Making a Pentagon

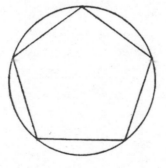

'I am about to start on making a silk patchwork quilt,' said a lady, 'all composed of pieces in the form of a pentagon. How am I to cut out a true pentagon in cardboard, the sides of which must measure exactly an inch? Of course, I can draw a circle, and then by trial with the compass find five points equidistant on the circumference' (see the illustration), 'but unless I know the correct size of my circle the pentagon is just as it happens, and the sides are always a little more, or a little less, than an exact inch.' Could you show her a simple and direct way of doing it without any trial?

21. Drawing an Oval

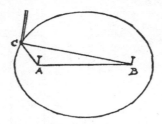

This trick for drawing an oval is very useful if you have to cut a mount for a portrait or to make an oval flower-bed. You drive in two pins or nails (or, in the case of the flower-bed, two stakes) and enclose them with an endless band of thread or string, as shown in our diagram, where the pins are at A and B, and the pencil point, at C, stretches the loop of thread. If you keep the thread taut and pass the pencil all round until you come back to the starting-point you will describe the perfect oval shown.

But I have sometimes heard the complaint that the method is too haphazard: that it was only by a lot of trials that you can draw an oval of the exact dimensions required. This is a delusion, and it will make an interesting little puzzle to show at what distance apart the pins should be placed, and what length the string should be, to draw an oval, say, twelve inches in length by eight inches in breadth. Can you discover the very simple rule for doing this?

22. With Compasses Only

Can you show how to mark off the four corners of a square, using a pair of compasses only? You simply use a sheet of paper and the compasses, and there is no trick, such as folding the paper.

23. Lines and Squares

With how few straight lines can you make exactly one hundred squares? Thus, in the first diagram it will be found that with nine straight lines I have made twenty squares (twelve with sides of the length A B, six with sides A C, and two with sides of the length A D). In the second diagram, although I use one more line, I only get seventeen squares. So, you see, everything depends on how the lines are drawn. Remember there must be exactly one hundred squares – neither more nor fewer.

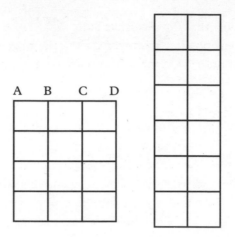

24. The Circle and Discs

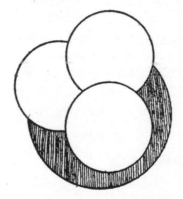

During a recent visit to a fair we saw a man with a table, on the oil-cloth covering of which was painted a large red circle, and he invited the public to cover this circle entirely with five tin discs which he provided, and offered a substantial prize to anybody who was successful. The circular discs were all of the same size, and each, of course, smaller than the red circle. The diagram, where three discs are shown placed, will make everything clear.

He showed that it was 'quite easy when you know how' by covering up the circle himself without any apparent difficulty, but many tried over and over again and failed every time. I should explain that it was a condition that when once you had placed any disc you were not allowed to shift it, otherwise, by sliding them about after they had been placed, it might be tolerably easy to do.

Let us assume that the red circle is six inches in diameter. Now, what is the smallest possible diameter (say, to the nearest half-inch) for the five discs in order to make a solution possible?

25.   Mr Grindle's Garden

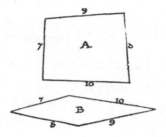

'My neighbour,' said Mr Grindle, 'generously offered me, for a garden, as much land as I could enclose with four straight walls measuring 7, 8, 9 and 10 rods in length respectively.'

'And what was the largest area you were able to enclose?' asked his friend.

Perhaps the reader can discover Mr Grindle's correct answer. You see, in the case of three sides the triangle can only enclose one area, but with four sides it is quite different. For example, it is obvious that the area of Diagram A is greater than that of B, though the sides are the same.

26. The Garden Path

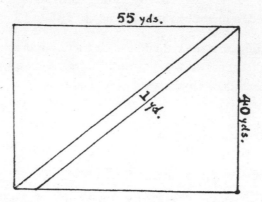

A man has a rectangular garden, 55 yds by 40 yds, and he makes a diagonal path, one yard wide, exactly in the manner indicated in the diagram. What is the area of the path? Dimensions for the garden are generally given that only admit of an approximate answer, but I select figures that will give an answer that is quite exact. The width of the path is exaggerated in the diagram for the sake of clearness.

27. The Garden Bed

Here is quite a simple little puzzle. A man has a triangular lawn of the proportions shown, and he wants to make the largest possible rectangular flower-bed without enclosing the tree. How is he to do it? This will serve to teach the uninitiated a simple rule that may prove useful on occasion. For example, it would equally apply to the case of a carpenter who had a triangular board and wished to cut out the largest possible rectangular table-top without including a bad knot in the wood.

28.   A Fence Problem

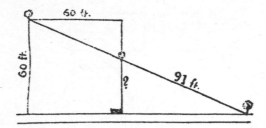

A man has a square field, 60 ft. by 60 ft., with other property, adjoining the highway. For some reason he put up a straight fence in the line of the three trees, as shown, and the length of fence from the middle tree to the tree on the road was just 91 feet. What is the distance in exact feet from the middle tree to the gate on the road?

29.   A New Match Puzzle

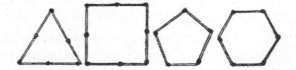

I have a box of matches. I find that I can form with them any given pair of these four regular figures, using all the matches every time. Thus, if there were eleven matches, I could form with them, as shown, the triangle and pentagon or the pentagon and hexagon, or the square and triangle (by using only three matches in the triangle); but could not with eleven matches form the triangle and hexagon, or the square and pentagon, or the square and hexagon. Of course there must be the same number of matches in every side of a figure. Now, what is the smallest number of matches I can have in the box?

30.   Hurdles and Sheep

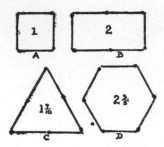

This is a little puzzle that you can try with matches. A farmer says that four of his hurdles will form a square enclosure just sufficient for one sheep. That being so, what is the smallest number of hurdles that he will require for enclosing ten sheep? Everything depends on the shape of your enclosure. The only other way of placing the four matches (or hurdles) in A is to form a diamond-shaped figure, and the more attenuated this diamond becomes the smaller will be its area, until the sides meet, when there will be no area enclosed at all. If you place six matches, as in B, you will have room for two sheep. But if you place them as in C, you will only have room for one sheep, for seven-tenths of a sheep will only exist as mutton. And if you place them as in D, you can still only accommodate two sheep, which is the maximum for six hurdles. Now, how many hurdles do you require for ten sheep?

31.   The Four Draughtsmen

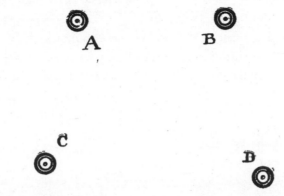

The four draughtsmen are shown exactly as they stood on a square chequered board – not necessarily eight squares by eight – but the ink with which the board was drawn was evanescent, so that all the diagram except the men has disappeared. How many squares were there in the board and how am I to reconstruct it? I know that each man stood in the middle of a square, one on the edge of each side of the board and no man in a corner. It is a real puzzle, until you hit on the method of solution, and then to get the correct answer is absurdly easy.

32.   A Crease Problem

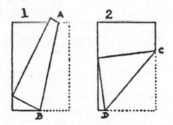

Fold a page, so that the bottom outside corner touches the inside edge and the crease is the shortest possible. That is about as simple a question as we could put, but it will puzzle a good many readers to discover just where to make that fold. I give two examples of folding. It will be seen that the crease AB is considerably longer than CD, but the latter is not the shortest possible.

33. The Six Submarines

If five submarines, sunk on the same day, all went down at the same spot where another had previously been sunk, how might they all lie at rest so that every one of the six U-boats should touch every other one? To simplify we will say, place six ordinary wooden matches so that every match shall touch every other match. No bending or breaking allowed.

34. Economy in String

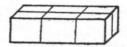

Owing to the scarcity of string a lady found herself in this dilemma. In making up a parcel for her son, she was limited to using 12 feet of string, exclusive of knots, which passed round the parcel once lengthways and twice round its girth, as shown in the illustration. What was the largest rectangular parcel that she could make up, subject to these conditions?

35. The Stone Pedestal

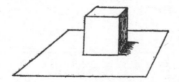

In laying the base and cubic pedestal for a certain public memorial, the stonemason used cubic blocks of stone all measuring one foot on every side. There was exactly the same number of these blocks (all uncut) in the pedestal as in the square base on the centre of which it stood. Look at the sketch and try to determine the total number of blocks actually used.

The base is only a single block in depth.

36. The Bricklayer's Task

When a man walled in his estate, one of the walls was partly level and partly over a small rise or hill, precisely as shown in the drawing herewith, wherein it will be observed that the distance from A to B is the same as from B to C. Now, the master-builder desired and claimed that he should be paid more for the part that was on the hill than for the part that was level, since (at least, so he held) it demanded the use of more material. But the employer insisted that he should pay less for that part. It was a nice point, over which they nearly had recourse to the law. Which of them was in the right?

37. A Cube Paradox

I had two solid cubes of lead, one very slightly larger than the other, just as shown in the illustration. Through one of them I cut a hole (without destroying the continuity of its four sides) so that the other cube could be passed right through it. On weighing them afterwards it was found that the larger cube was still the heavier of the two! How was this possible?

38.   The Cardboard Box

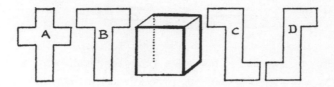

Readers must have often remarked on the large number of little things that one would have expected to have been settled generations ago, and yet never appear to have been considered. Here is a case that has just occurred to me. If I have a closed cubical cardboard box, by running the penknife along seven of the twelve edges (it must always be seven) I can lay it out in one flat piece in various shapes. Thus, in the diagram, if I pass the knife along the darkened edges and down the invisible edge indicated by the dotted line, I get the shape A. Another way of cutting produces B or C. It will be seen that D is simply C turned over, so we will not call that a different shape. Now, how many different shapes can be produced?

39.   The Austrian Pretzel

Here is a twisted Vienna bread roll, known as a Pretzel. The twist, like the curl in a pig's tail, is entirely for ornament. The Wiener Pretzel, like some other things, is doomed to be cut up or broken, and the interest lies in the number of resultant pieces. Suppose you had the Pretzel depicted in the illustration lying on the table before you, what is the greatest number of pieces into which you could cut it with a single straight cut of a knife? In what direction would you make the cut?

40. Cutting the Cheese

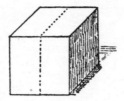

Here is a simple question that will require just a few moments' thought to get an exact answer. I have a piece of cheese in the shape of a cube. How am I to cut it in two pieces with one straight cut of the knife so that the two new surfaces produced by the cut shall each be a perfect hexagon? Of course, if cut in the direction of the dotted line the surfaces would be squares. Now produce hexagons.

41. A Tree-planting Puzzle

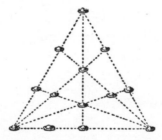

A man planted thirteen trees in the manner shown, and so formed eight straight rows with four trees in every row. But he was not satisfied with that second tree in the horizontal row. As he quaintly put it, 'it was not doing enough work – seemed to be a sort of loafer.' It certainly does appear to be somewhat out of the game, as the only purpose it serves is to complete one row. So he set to work on a better arrangement, and in the end discovered that he could plant thirteen trees so as to get nine rows of four. Can the reader show how it might be done?

42.   The Way to Tipperary

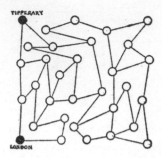

The popular bard assures us that 'it is a long, long way to Tipperary.'
Look at the accompanying chart and see if you can discover the best
way from London to 'the sweetest girl I know.' The lines represent
stages from town to town, and it is necessary to get from London to
Tipperary in an even number of stages. You will find no difficulty in
getting there in 3, 5, 7, 9 or 11 stages, but these are odd numbers and
will not do. The reason they are odd is that they all omit the sea
passage, a very necessary stage. If you get to your destination in an
even number of stages, it will be because you have crossed the Irish
Sea. Which stage is the Irish Sea?

43.   Marking a Tennis Court

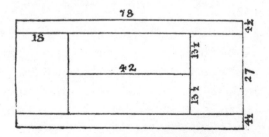

The lines of our tennis court are faint and want re-marking. My
marker is of such a kind that, though I can start anywhere and finish
anywhere, it cannot be lifted off the lines when working without
making a mess. I have therefore to go over some of the lines twice.
Where should I start and what route should I take, without lifting the
marker, to mark the court completely and yet go over the minimum
distance twice? I give the correct proportions of a tennis court in feet.
What is the best route?

44. The Nine Bridges

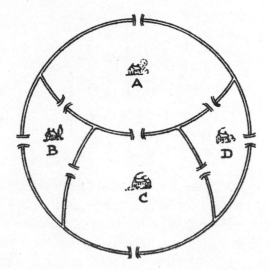

The illustration represents the map of a district with a peculiar system of irrigation. The lines are waterways enclosing the four islands, A, B, C, and D, each with its house, and it will be seen that there are nine bridges available. Whenever Tompkins leaves his house to visit his friend Johnson, who lives in one of the others, he always carries out the eccentric rule of crossing every one of the bridges once, and once only, before arriving at his destination. How many different routes has he to select from? You may choose any house you like as the residence of Tompkins.

45. The Five Regiments

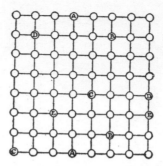

The illustration represents a map (considerably simplified for our purpose) of a certain district. The circles are towns and the lines roads. During the war five regiments marched to new positions on the same night. The body stationed at the upper A marched to the lower A, that at the upper B to the lower B, that at the upper C to the lower C, that at the upper D to the lower D, and the regiment at the left-hand E marched to the right-hand E. Yet no regiment ever saw anything of any other regiment. Can you mark out the route taken by each so that no two regiments ever go along the same road anywhere?

46. Going to Church

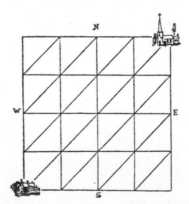

A man living in the house shown in the diagram wants to know what is the greatest number of different routes by which he can go to the church. The possible roads are indicated by the lines, and he always walks either due N, due E or NE; that is, he goes so that every step brings him nearer to the church. Can you count the total number of different routes from which he may select?

47. A Motor-car Puzzle

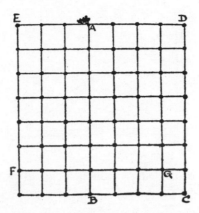

A traveller starts in his car from the point A and wishes to go as far as possible while making only fifteen turnings, and never going along the same road twice. The dots represent towns and are one mile apart. Supposing, for example, that he went straight to B, then straight to C, then to D, E, F and G, then you will find that he has gone 37 miles in five turnings. How far can he go in fifteen turnings?

48. The Fly and the Honey

I have a cylindrical cup four inches high and six inches in circumference. On the inside of the vessel, one inch from the top, is a drop of honey, and on the opposite side of the vessel, one inch from the bottom on the outside, is a fly. Can you tell exactly how far the fly must walk to reach the honey?

49.   The Russian Motor-cyclists

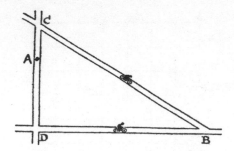

Two Army motor-cyclists, on the road at Adjbkmlprzll, wish to go to Brczrtwxy, which, for the sake of brevity, are marked in the accompanying map as A and B. Now, Pipipoff said: 'I shall go to D, which is six miles, and then take the straight road to B, another fifteen miles.' But Sliponsky thought he would try the upper road by way of C. Curiously enough, they found on reference to their cyclometers that the distance either way was exactly the same. This being so, they ought to have been able easily to answer the General's simple question, 'How far is it from A to C?' It can be done in the head in a few moments, if you only know how. Can the reader state correctly the distance?

50.   Those Russian Cyclists Again

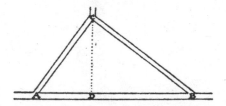

Here is another little experience of the two Russian Army motor-cyclists that I described in our last puzzle. In the section from a map given in our illustration we are shown three long straight roads, forming a right-angled triangle. The General asked the two men how far it was from A to B. Pipipoff replied that all he knew was that in riding right round the triangle, from A to B, from there to C and home to A, his cyclometer registered exactly sixty miles, while Sliponsky could only say that he happened to know that C was exactly twelve miles from the road A to B – that is, to the point D, as shown by the dotted line. Whereupon the General made a very simple calculation in his head and declared that the distance from A to B must be—— Can the reader discover so easily how far it was?

51.   The Despatch-rider in Flanders

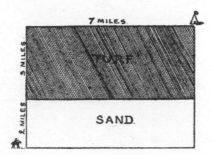

A despatch-rider on horseback, somewhere in Flanders, had to ride with all possible speed from the position in which he is shown to the spot indicated by the tent. The distances are marked on the plan. Now, he can ride just twice as fast over the soft turf (the shaded ground) as he can ride over the loose sand. Can you show what is the quickest possible route for him to take? Of course, the turf and the sand extend for miles to the right and the left with the same respective depths of three miles and two miles, so there is no trick in the puzzle.

52. **Land Division**

A father has a square of land. He divides it so as to reserve to himself one-fourth in the form of a square; thus,

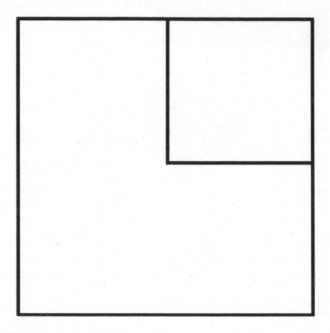

He has four sons, and divides the remainder among his sons in such a way that each son will share equally with his brother, and in similar shape. How was his farm divided?

53. **The Orchard**

Plant an orchard of twenty-one trees, so that there shall be nine straight rows, with five trees in each row, the outline a regular geometrical figure, and the trees all at unequal distances from each other.

54. **Drawing an Oval**

Can you describe an oval with one sweep of the compasses?

55.   The Four Householders

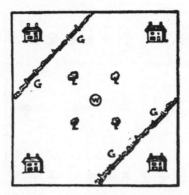

Here is a square plot of land with four houses, four trees, a well (W) in the centre, and hedges planted across with four gateways (G).

Can you divide the ground so that each householder shall have an equal portion of land, one tree, one gateway, an equal length of hedge, and free access to the well without trespass?

56.   The Five Fences

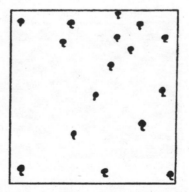

A man owned a large, square, fenced-in field in which were sixteen oak trees, as depicted in the illustration. He wished, for some eccentric reason, to put up five straight fences, so that every tree should be in a separate enclosure.

How did he do it? Just take your pencil and draw five straight strokes across the field, so that every tree shall be fenced off from all the others.

57. The Farmer's Sons

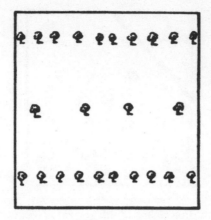

A farmer once had a square piece of ground on which stood twenty-four trees, exactly as shown in the illustration. He left instructions in his will that each of his eight sons should receive the same amount of ground and the same number of trees. How was the land to be divided in the simplest possible manner?

58. Avoiding the Mines

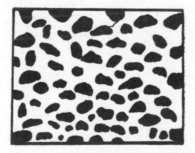

Here we have a portion of the North Sea thickly sown with mines by the enemy. A cruiser made a safe passage through them from south to north in two straight courses, without striking a single mine. Take your pencil and try to discover how it is done. Go from the bottom of the chart to any point you like on the chart in a straight line, and then from that point to the top in another straight line without touching a mine.

59.   Six Straight Fences

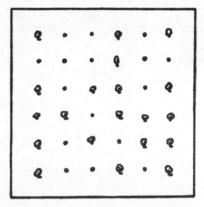

A man had a small plantation of thirty-six trees, planted in the form of a square. Some of these died and had to be cut down in the positions indicated by the dots in our illustration. How is it possible to put up six straight fences across the field, so that every one of the remaining twenty trees shall be in a separate enclosure? As a matter of fact, twenty-two trees might be so enclosed by six straight fences if their positions were a little more accommodating, but we have to deal with the trees as they stand in regular formation, which makes all the difference.

Just take your pencil and see if you can make six straight lines across the field so as to leave every tree separately enclosed.

60.   Footprints in the Snow

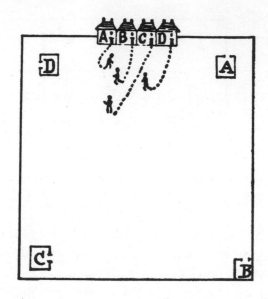

Four schoolboys, living respectively in the houses A, B, C and D, attended different schools. After a snowstorm one morning their footprints were examined, and it was found that no boy had ever crossed the track of another boy, or gone outside the square boundary. Take your pencil and continue their tracks, so that the boy A goes to the school A, the boy B to the school B, and so on, without any line crossing another line.

Chapter 4. Logical and Lateral Thinking Puzzles

1. ## Crossing the Ferry

Six persons, all related, have to cross a river in a small boat that will only hold two. Mr Webster, who had to plan the little affair, had quarrelled with his father-in-law and his son, and, I am sorry to say, Mrs Webster was not on speaking terms with her own mother or her daughter-in-law. In fact, the relations were so strained that it was not safe to permit any of the belligerents to pass over together or to remain together on the same side of the river. And to prevent further discord, no man was to be left with two women or two men with three women. How are they to perform the feat in the fewest possible crossings? No tricks, such as making use of a rope or current, or swimming across, are allowed.

2. ## Missionaries and Cannibals

There is a strange story of three missionaries and three cannibals, who had to cross a river in a small boat that would only carry two men at a time. Being acquainted with the peculiar appetites of the cannibals, the missionaries could never allow their companions to be in a majority on either side of the river. Only one of the missionaries and one of the cannibals could row the boat. How did they manage to get across?

3.   A Domino Square

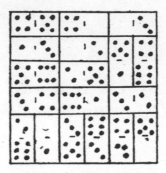

Select any eighteen dominoes you please from an ordinary box, and arrange them any way you like in a square so that no number shall be repeated in any row or any column. The example given is imperfect, for it will be seen that though no number is repeated in any one of the columns yet three of the rows break the condition. There are two 4's and two blanks in the first row, two 5's and two 6's in the third row, and two 3's in the fourth row. Can you form an arrangement without such errors? Blank counts as a number.

4.   A Domino Star

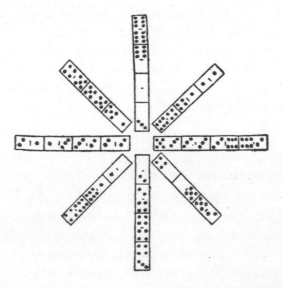

Place the twenty-eight dominoes, as shown in the illustration, so as to form a star with alternate rays of four and three dominoes. Every ray must contain twenty-one pips (in the example only one ray contains this number) and the central numbers must be 1, 2, 3, 4, 5, 6, and two blanks, as at present, and these may be in any order. In every ray the dominoes must be placed according to the ordinary rule, six against six, blank against blank, and so on.

5.   Domino Groups

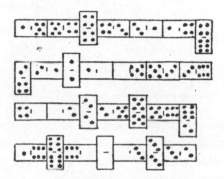

I wonder how many readers know that if you lay out the twenty-eight dominoes in line according to the ordinary rule – six against six, two against two, blank against blank, and so on – the last number must always be the same as the first, so that they will really always form a circle. It is a very ancient trick to conceal one domino (but do not take a double) and then ask him to arrange all the others in line without your seeing. It will astonish him when you tell him, after he has succeeded, what the two end numbers are. They must be those on the domino that you have withdrawn, for that domino completes the circle. If the dominoes are laid out in the manner shown in our illustration and I then break the line into four lengths of seven dominoes each, it will be found that the sum of the pips in the first group is 49, in the second 34, in the third 46, and in the fourth 39. Now I want to play them out so that all the four groups of seven when the line is broken shall contain the same number of pips. Can you find a way of doing it?

6.   Les Quadrilles

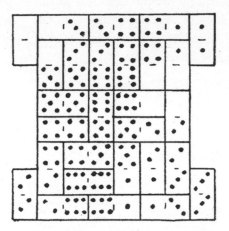

This old French puzzle will, I think, be found very interesting. It is required to arrange a complete set of twenty-eight dominoes so as to form the figure shown in our illustration, with all the numbers forming a series of squares. Thus, in the upper two rows we have a square of blanks, and a square of four 3's, and a square of 4's and a square of 1's; in the third and fourth rows we have squares of 5, 6 and blank, and so on. This is, in fact, a perfect solution under the conditions usually imposed, but what I now ask for is an arrangement with no blanks anywhere on the outer edge. At present every number from blank to 6 inclusive will be found somewhere on the margin. Can you construct an arrangement with all the blanks inside?

7.   A Puzzle with Cards

Take from the pack the thirteen cards forming the suit of diamonds and arrange them in this order face downwards with the 3 at the top and 5 at the bottom: 3, 8, 7, ace, queen, 6, 4, 2, jack, king, 10, 9, 5. Now play them out in a row on the table in this way. As you spell 'ace' transfer for each letter a card from the top to the bottom of the pack – A-C-E – and play the fourth card on to the table. Then spell T-W-O, while transferring three more cards to the bottom, and place the next card on the table. Then spell T-H-R-E-E, while transferring five to the bottom, and so on until all are laid out in a row, and you will find they will be all in regular order. Of course, you will spell out the knave as J-A-C-K. Can you arrange the whole pack so that they will play out correctly in order, first all the diamonds, then the hearts, then the spades, and lastly the clubs?

8.   A Card Trick

Take an ordinary pack of playing-cards and regard all the court cards as tens. Now, look at the top card – say it is a seven – place it on the table face downwards and play more cards on top of it, counting up to twelve. Thus, the bottom card being seven, the next will be eight, the next nine, and so on, making six cards in that pile. Then look again at the top card of the pack – say it is a queen – then count 10, 11, 12 (three cards in all), and complete the second pile. Continue this, always counting up to twelve, and if at last you have not sufficient cards to complete a pile, put these apart. Now, if I am told how many piles have been made and how many unused cards remain over, I can at once tell you the sum of all the bottom cards in the piles. I simply multiply by 13 the number of piles less 4, and add the number of cards left over. Thus, if there were 6 piles and 5 cards over, then 13 times 2 (i.e. 6 less 4) added to 5 equals 31, the sum of the bottom cards. Why is this? That is the question.

9.   A Golf Competition Puzzle

I was asked to construct some schedules for players in American golf competitions. The conditions are: (1) Every player plays every other player once, and once only. (2) There are half as many links as players, and every player plays twice on every links except one, on which he plays but once. (3) All the players play simultaneously in every round, and the last round is the one in which every player is playing on a links for the first time. I have written out schedules for a long series of even numbers of players up to twenty-six, but the problem is too difficult for this page except in its most simple form – for six players. Can the reader, calling the players A, B, C, D, E, and F, and pairing these in all possible ways, such as A B, C D, E F, A F, B D, C E, etc., complete the simple little table below for six players? For such a small number it is easy but interesting.

	ROUNDS				
	1	2	3	4	5
1ST LINKS					
2ND LINKS					
3RD LINKS					

10. Cricket Scores

In a country match Great Muddleton, who went in first, made a score of which they were proud. Then Little Wurzleford had their innings and scored a quarter less. The Muddletonians in their next attempt made a quarter less than their opponents, who, curiously enough, were only rewarded on their second effort by a quarter less than the last score. Thus, every innings was a quarter less fruitful in runs than the one that preceded it. Yet the Muddletonians won the match by fifty runs. Can you give the exact score for every one of the four innings?

11. Football Results

Near the close of a football season a correspondent informed me that when he was returning from Glasgow after the international match between Scotland and England the following table caught his eye in a newspaper:

	Played	Won	Lost	Drawn	Goals For	Against	Points
Scotland . .	3	3	0	0	7	1	6
England . .	3	1	1	1	2	3	3
Wales . .	3	1	1	1	3	3	3
Ireland . .	3	0	3	0	1	6	0

As he knew, of course, that Scotland had beaten England by 3 – 0 it struck him that it might be possible to find the scores in the other five matches from the table. In this he succeeded. Can you discover from it how many goals were won, drawn, or lost by each side in every match?

12.   Noughts and Crosses

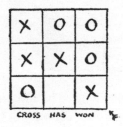

CROSS HAS WON

Every child knows how to play this ancient game. You make a square of nine cells, and each of the two players, playing alternately, puts his mark (a nought or a cross, as the case may be) in a cell with the object of getting three in a line. Whichever player gets three in a line wins. Between two players who thoroughly understand the play every game should be drawn, for neither party could ever win except through the blundering of his opponent. Can you prove this? Can you be sure of not losing a game against an expert opponent?

13.   The Horse-shoe Game

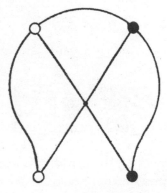

This little game is an interesting companion to our 'Noughts and Crosses'. There are two players. One has two white counters, the other two black. Playing alternately, each places a counter on a vacant point, where he leaves it. When all are played, you slide only, and the player is beaten who is so blocked that he cannot move. In the example, Black has just placed his lower counter. White now slides his lower one to the centre, and wins. Black should have played to the centre himself, and won. Now, which player ought to win at this game?

14. Turning the Die

This is played with a single die. The first player calls any number he chooses, from 1 to 6, and the second player throws the die at hazard. Then they take it in turns to roll over the die in any direction they choose, but never giving it more than a quarter turn. The score increases as they proceed, and the player wins who manages to score 25 or force his opponent to score beyond 25. I will give an example game. A calls 6, and B happens to throw a 3 (as shown in our illustration), making the score 9. Now A decides to turn up 1, scoring 10; B turns up 3, scoring 13; A turns up 6, scoring 19; B turns up 3, scoring 22; A turns up 1, scoring 23; and B turns up 2, scoring 25 and winning.

What call should A make in order to have the best chance of winning? Remember that the numbers on opposite sides of a correct die always sum to 7, that is, 1 – 6, 2 – 5, 3 – 4.

15. The Three Dice

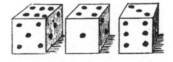

Mason and Jackson were playing with three dice. The player won whenever the numbers thrown added up to one of two numbers he selected at the beginning of the game. As a matter of fact, Mason selected seven and thirteen, and one of his winning throws is shown in the illustration. What were his chances of winning a throw? And what two other numbers should Jackson have selected for his own throws to make his chances of winning exactly equal?

16. The 37 Puzzle Game

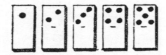

Place the five dominoes, 1, 2, 3, 4, 5, on the table. There are two players, who play alternately. The first player places a coin on any domino, say the 5, which scores 5; then the second player removes the coin to another domino, say to the 3, and adds that domino, scoring 8; then the first player removes the coin again, say to the 1, scoring 9; and so on. The player who scores 37, or forces his opponent to score more than 37, wins. Remember, the coin must be removed to a different domino at each play. How can I play and be certain to win?

17. The Twenty-two Game

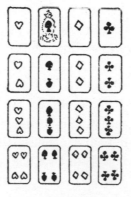

Lay out the sixteen cards as shown. Two players alternately turn down a card and add it to the common score, and the player who makes the score of twenty-two, or forces his opponent to go beyond that number, wins. For example, A turns down a 4, B turns down a 3 (counting 7), A turns down a 4 (counting 11), B plays a 2 (counting 13), A plays 1 (14), B plays 3 (17), and whatever A does, B scores the winning 22 next play. Again, supposing the play was 3 – 1, 1 – 2, 3 – 3, 1 – 2, 1 – 4, scoring 21, the second player would win again, because there is no 1 left and his opponent must go beyond 22. Now, which player should always win, and how?

18. The Nine Squares Game

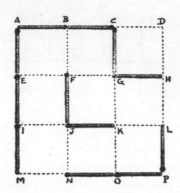

Make the simple square diagram shown and provide a box of matches. The side of the large square is three matches in length. The game is, playing one match at a time alternately, to enclose more of those small squares than your opponent. For every small square that you enclose you not only score one point, but you play again. The illustration shows an illustrative game in progress. Twelve matches are placed, my opponent and myself having made six plays each, and, as I had first play, it is now my turn to place a match. What is my best line of play in order to win most squares? If I play F G my opponent will play B F and score one point. Then, as he has the right to play again, he will score another with E F and again with I J, and still again with G K. If he now plays C D, I have nothing better than D H (scoring one), but, as I have to play again, I am compelled, whatever I do, to give him all the rest. So he will win by 8 to 1 – a bad defeat for me. Now, what should I have played instead of that disastrous F G? There is room for a lot of skilful play in the game, and it can never end in a draw.

19.   A Wheel Fallacy

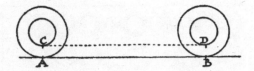

Here is a curious fallacy that I have found to be very perplexing to many people. The wheel shown in the illustration makes one complete revolution in passing from A to B. It is therefore obvious that the line (A B) is exactly equal in length to the circumference of the wheel. What that length is cannot be stated with accuracy for any diameter, but we can get it near enough for all practical purposes. Thus, if it is a bicycle wheel with a diameter of 28 inches, we can multiply by 22 and divide by 7, and get the length – 88 inches. This is a trifle too much, but if we multiply by 355 and divide by 113 we get 87.9646, which is nearer; or by multiplying by 3.1416 we get 87.9648, which is still more nearly exact. This is just by the way.

Now the inner circle (the large hub in the illustration) also makes one complete revolution along the imaginary dotted line (C D) and, since the line (C D) is equal to the line (A B), the circumference of the larger and smaller circles are the same! This is certainly not true, as the merest child can see at a glance. Yet, wherein lies the fallacy? Try to think it out. There can be no question that the hub makes one complete revolution in passing from C to D. Then why does not C D equal in length its circumference?

20. A Chain Puzzle

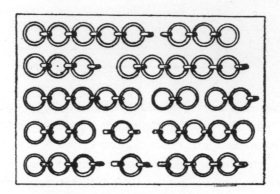

A man has eighty links of old chain in thirteen fragments, as shown here. It will cost him 1d. to open a link and 2d. to weld one together again. What is the lowest price it must cost him to join all the pieces together so as to form an endless chain?

A new chain will cost him 3s. What is the cheapest method of procedure? Remember that the large and small links must run alternately.

21. The Six Pennies

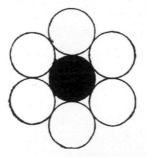

Lay six pennies on the table, and then arrange them as shown by the six white circles in the illustration, so that if a seventh penny (the black circle) were produced it could be dropped in the centre and exactly touch each of the six. It is required to get it exact, without any dependence on the eye. In this case you are not allowed to lift any penny off the table – otherwise there would be no puzzle at all – nor can any measuring or marking be employed. You require only the six pennies.

22. Folding Postage Stamps

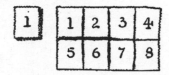

If you have eight postage stamps, 4 by 2, as in the diagram, it is very interesting to discover the various ways in which they can be folded so that they will lie under one stamp, as shown. I will say at once that they can actually be folded in forty different ways so that No. 1 is face upwards and all the others invisible beneath it. Nos. 5, 2, 7 and 4 will always be face downwards, but you may arrange for any stamp except No. 6 to lie next to No. 1, though there are only two ways each in which Nos. 7 and 8 can be brought into that position. From a little law that I discovered, I was convinced that they could be folded in the order 1, 5, 6, 4, 8, 7, 3, 2, and also 1, 3, 7, 5, 6, 8, 4, 2, with No. 1 at the top, face upwards, but it puzzled me for some time to discover how. Can the reader so fold them without, of course, tearing any of the perforation? Try it with a piece of paper well creased like the diagram, and number the stamps on both sides for convenience. It is a fascinating puzzle. Do not give it up as impossible!

23. An Ingenious Match Puzzle

Place six matches as shown, and then shift one match without touching the others so that the new arrangement shall represent an arithmetical fraction equal to 1. The match forming the horizontal fraction bar must not be the one moved.

24. Fifty-seven to Nothing

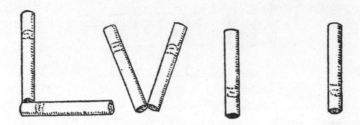

After the last puzzle, this one should be easy.

It will be seen that we have arranged six cigarettes so as to represent the number 57. The puzzle is to remove any two of them you like (without disturbing any of the others) and so replace them as to represent 0, or nothing. Remember that you can only shift two cigarettes. There are two entirely different solutions. Can you find one or both?

25. The Five Squares

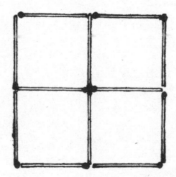

It will be seen that the twelve matches are so arranged that they form four squares. Can you rearrange the same number of matches (all lying flat on the table) so that they enclose five squares? Every square must be entirely 'empty' or the illustration itself will show five squares if we were allowed to count the large square forming the boundary. No duplicated match or loose ends are allowed.

26. A Calendar Puzzle

Under our present calendar rules, the first day of a century can never fall on a Sunday or a Wednesday or a Friday. Can you explain the mystery in as simple a way as possible?

Note that 1901 was the first day of a century: not 1900.

27. The Fly's Tour

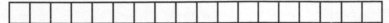

I had a ribbon of paper, divided into squares on each side, as shown in the illustration. I joined the two ends together to make a ring, which I threw on the table. Later I noticed that a fly pitched on the ring and walked in a line over every one of the squares on both sides, returning to the point from which it started, *without ever passing over the edge of the paper!* Its course passed through the centres of the squares all the time. How was this possible?

28. A Musical Enigma

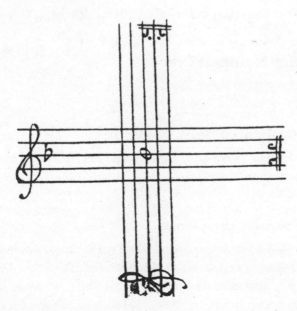

What composer does this German musical diagram represent?

29. An Arithmetic Puzzle

Place three 6s together so as to amount to 7.

30. A Digital Puzzle

Place three 2s together so as to make 24.

31. A Mathematical Puzzle

Place three 3s together so as to make 24.

32. A Numeral Puzzle

Take one from nine and make it ten.

33. Another Numeral Puzzle

Add one to nine and make it twenty.

34. A Numeral Proof

Prove that one taken from nineteen leaves twenty.

35. Another Numeral Proof

Prove that half of eleven is six.

36. A Complicated Sum

How would you take nine from six and ten from nine and fifty from forty, so that six remains?

37. The Fox and the Goose

A man with a fox, a goose, and some corn, came to a river which it was necessary to cross. He could, however, take only one of the three across at a time, and if he left the goose and corn while he took the fox over, the goose would eat the corn; but if he left the fox and goose, the fox would kill the goose. How did he get them all safely over?

38.   A Lodging-house Difficulty

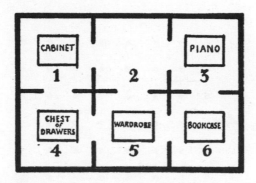

The Dobsons secured apartments at Slocomb-on-Sea. There were six
rooms on the same floor, all communicating, as shown in the diagram.
The rooms they took were numbers 4, 5 and 6, all facing the sea. But
a little difficulty arose. Mr Dobson insisted that the piano and the
bookcase should change rooms. This was wily, for the Dobsons were
not musical, but they wanted to prevent anyone else playing the
instrument. Now, the rooms were very small and the pieces of
furniture indicated were very big, so that no two of these articles could
be got into any room at the same time. How was the exchange to be
made with the least possible labour? Suppose, for example, you first
move the wardrobe into No. 2, then you can move the bookcase into
No. 5, and the piano to No. 6, and so on. It is a fascinating puzzle, but
the landlady had reasons for not appreciating it. Try to solve her
difficulty in the fewest possible removals with counters or coins on a
sheet of paper.

39.   Minesweeping

A minesweeper, starting from the position shown in the illustration, picks up all the sixty-four mines in fourteen straight courses.

The seventh course must end at the large mine, and the fourteenth must end at the point from which she sets out. Take your pencil and try to strike out all the mines in fourteen continuous straight strokes under the conditions. A solution in fifteen strokes is not difficult to find, but to perform the feat in fourteen requires skilful seamanship.

40.   The Cyclist's Journey

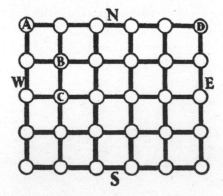

The illustration represents a route map, put into a simplified form for puzzle purposes. The circles are towns and villages, and the lines the roads that connect them. A cyclist, setting out from A, proposed to visit a certain town, and he amused himself by working out the number of different routes by which he could go if he always cycled either due east or due south. He found that there were exactly twenty-one different routes and no more. Now, which town was he going to visit? You see, if he were going to B, there are two routes; if he were going to C, there are three routes, and if he were going to D, there is only one straight route – for he never rides northward or westward. Can you point out his destination?

41.   The Rotator Puzzle

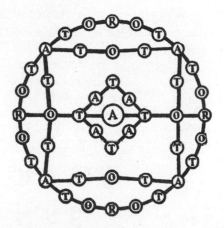

What is the total number of different ways in which the word ROTATOR can be spelt out in the illustration? You can start at any R and go up and down, in and out, backwards or forwards, so long as you always pass from one letter to another that adjoins it on a line. To count them all in rotation – 'One, two, three, four, five,' etc. – is not practicable, for you cannot possibly remember which routes you have counted and which you have not, so you will be sure to get either omissions or repetitions, or both. You must bear in mind the symmetrical character of the formation and proceed on some system. Thus, if you know the number of routes starting from the R at the top, you need not count those from the other R's, for the result must be the same. This should suggest other short cuts to the solution.

42.   The Ten Counters

Here is a little puzzle that may keep you amused for some time, though it is quite possible that you may hit on the answer at once. Place ten counters, or coins, on the table in two straight lines of five, as shown in the illustration. Now, take up four of them (any four you like) and replace them so that the ten counters shall form five straight rows with four counters in every row.

43.   Cryptic Addition

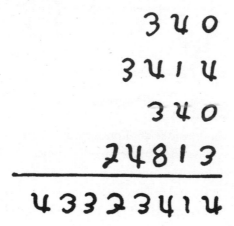

Can you prove that the above addition sum is correct?

44. Cupid's Arithmetic

15122 11116 9601621

Dora Crackham one morning produced a slip of paper bearing the jumble of figures shown in our illustration. She said that a young mathematician had this poser presented to him by his betrothed when she was in a playful mood.

'What am I to do with it?' asked George.

'Just interpret its meaning,' she replied. 'If it is properly regarded it should not be difficult to decipher.'

Chapter 5. Word Puzzles

1. A Motto Puzzle

Here is a little puzzle that ought not to be difficult for anyone to solve with a little thought and patience. Place the point of your pencil on one of the letters, and then in a continuous sequence, always passing from a square to another adjoining it (either laterally or diagonally), spell out a very well-known motto or proverb. When I add that if you start at the Y, you might proceed Y A N C, or if you started at the C, you could read C A Y N, and so on, there can be no possible misunderstanding of the conditions.

Y	N	E	B	H
A	C	H	T	R
M	**O**	**T**	**T**	**O**
O	O	O	P	L
K	S	S	I	O

2. Numerical Enigma

I am composed of seven letters and my whole is a plant.

My 1, 2 is a preposition.

My 5, 4, 3 is a kind of carriage.

My 3, 2, 7, 1 is something worn.

My 6, 7 means partnership.

3.   Beheadings

The ship rode in an . . . . bay;

Asleep . . . . . . the master lay;

A . . . . . and rugged man was he,

And like the . . . . at home at sea.

He like the . . . swooped on his prey,

Whene'er the . . came his way.

But now, while . the needle kept,

Forgetting all he lay and slept.

Behead the first missing word to make the second, behead the second word to make the third, and so on throughout.

4.   The Nine-letter Puzzle

Arrange nine letters of the alphabet thus:

D	O	N
A	R	T
B	E	Y

The puzzle is to get the largest number possible of readings of three-letter words in a straight line. You may use the same letter more than once, but repetitions of the same word do not count. In the example given we get the words DON, NOD, DAB, BAD, ART, BEY, ORE and DRY – eight in all. This can be easily beaten. What is the best you can do? They should all be English dictionary words.

5.   Making a Word Square

The puzzle is to form a word square by exchanging every letter once with another that is connected with it by a chess knight's move. Thus, taking the top row, you might exchange T with E, O with R, A with M, and so on. But a little thought will greatly simplify the task. Thus, as there is only one O, one L, and one N, these must clearly be transferred to the diagonal from the top left-hand corner to the bottom right-hand corner. Then, as the letters in the first row must be the same as in the first file, in the second row as in the second file, and so on, you are generally limited in your choice of making a pair. The puzzle can therefore be solved in a very few minutes.

T	O	A	Y	S	M
S	H	L	T	T	H
R	E	A	M	S	E
R	S	E	E	M	R
R	S	R	Y	S	T
E	I	N	E	M	I

6.   A Paradox

Four jolly men sat down to play,

And played all night till break of day.

They played for gold and not for fun,

With separate scores for every one.

Yet when they came to square accounts,

They all had made quite fair amounts.

Can you the paradox explain,

If no one lost, how could all gain?

7.   A Palindrome Puzzle

I do not believe there are in the English language more than about fifty or sixty palindromes – words that read backwards and forwards alike. Here are nine such palindromes: Aha! deed, hah! mum, nun, oxo, pip, redder, toot. Now I propose as a little puzzle that the reader tries to find longer palindromes beginning and ending with the same letters – a, d, h, etc. There is a longer word to fit every case. Proper nouns may be used.

8.   Building a Word Square

```
P   O   I   S   E   D
O   T   P   I   T   A
I   P   U   T   O   R
S   I   T   T   E   R
E   T   O   E   L   E
D   A   R   R   E   M
```

This would be a word square, if only all the lines and columns spelt real words which, with the exceptions of 'poised' and 'sitter,' they do not. The puzzle is to rearrange these letters so that a perfect word square may be formed. As a clue I will state that all the letters in the diagonal—P, T, U, T, L, M—are correctly placed as they stand at present. Most of the other letters are out of their proper places.

9.   A Word Square

'Come, let us sit beneath my *fifth*
    And drink a hearty *first*.
The hunt is done, my *second* slain,
    Th' excited crowd dispersed.'
But one with *fourth* of pity 'gan to plead,
    'Better if we could *third* the wanton deed.'
The five words form a word square.

10. Natural History

Tompkins: 'I say, Nobbs, speaking of horses, which has most legs – a horse or no horse?

Nobbs: 'Which has most legs?'

Tompkins: 'Yes, that's the question. Which has most legs – a horse or no horse?'

Nobbs: 'What a ridiculous question to ask a fellow. Of course, it stands to reason that – '

And yet Nobbs laughed when he heard his friend's answer to this curious question.

11. A Rebus

Here is a little enigma that may interest some of my readers:

> Whether backwards or forwards I'm read
>> It matters to me not a bit.
> I am gentle and light, and transposed
>> I am ever ready and fit.

12. Missing Words

Her cheek —— sadly, and there comes

   A sudden rush of tears,

As memory —— back across

   The —— of fleeting years.

She hears again the —— of love

   He made beneath this tree;

The merry —— ring in her ears.

   A widow now is she.

Every missing word contains the same five letters.

13. A Buried Quotation

In the following couplet there are two buried towns:

> In love inconstant I no pleasure find;
>
> No fickle girl is bonny to my mind.

Here, if you start at the 'c' in 'inconstant', you get the word 'Constantinople,' and beginning with the 'l' in 'girl' you have the second word, 'Lisbon.' Now in the following paragraph is concealed a familiar quotation from Shakespeare, each word being buried in its proper order. Can you discover the sentence?

'Strange weather! What could equal it? Yesterday sunshine and soft breezes; today a summer cyclone raging noisily; then other changes, as floods of the fiercest rain eddy beneath the blast.'

14. A Buried Proverb

In each of the following sentences a word is concealed, just as 'Blighty' is hidden in the sentence, 'Job, *light* your candle.' Read them in the order given and they will form a very familiar proverb:

1. A naughty cat ran away. 2. They found a closely written roll in gathering up the rubbish. 3. It is the best one that I have ever seen. 4. The rug at her stairway is not a valuable one. 5. He is an old acquaintance of mine. 6. Amos soon saw through the stratagem.

15. Thrice Beheaded

Untouched I tell of budding growth and life;

   Beheaded I lead upward more or less;

Again – with varied fragrance I am rife;

   Again – but little value I express.

16. A Charade

My *first* is possessed by the queen,

   May Providence long smile upon her!

My *next* at her court may be seen

   By those whom she chooses to honour.

My *whole,* 'tis admitted by all, gentle reader,

In learning and literature stands as a leader.

17. An Enigma

Just equal are my head and tail,

   My middle slender as can be.

Whether I stand on head or heel,

   Is all the same to you or me.

But if my head should be cut off,

   The matter true, although quite strange,

My head and body, severed thus,

   Will then at once to nothing change.

18. A Charade

View yonder smiling, bonny lass;

   My *first* sometimes she's reckoned,

And you will notice as we pass

   Her cheeks outvie my *second.*

Around her cottage in the spring

   My *whole* you may discover,

Like her, a simple, modest thing,

   With many an ardent lover.

19. A Charade

When Kate, the cook, prepared the meal,
   My *first* was in request;
My *next* is seen in lamb and veal,
   A quarter or a breast –
Which, with my *whole*, the table graced,
   And truly 'twas no wonder,
When at the board each guest was placed,
   To see my *third* thrown under.

20. A Charade

My *first* in the garden luxuriant grows,
Delicious and sweet, as everyone knows.
My *second*, a noisy, vain, quarrelsome thing,
The lord of a harem, as proud as a king.
My *whole* is still prouder, and seems to rejoice
As much in his tail as he does in his voice.

21. A Rebus

I am fat and well favoured
   When made up complete,
Curtail and you'll find me
   Quite wholesome to eat.
Restore me my tail, and
   In lieu take my head;
Like feathers I'm light,
   Or as heavy as lead.

22. **A Charade**

My *first* leaves no record to tell of its lot
But this simple fact, that it was and is not.
Cold and hard is my *second*, till touched by a flame,
The result of which is that it changes its name.
Many shrink from my *whole*, others labour to gain it,
And merit it least when they pant to obtain it.

23. **An Enigma**

I am a word of seven letters.
My 3rd, 4th, 5th and 7th are what the happy feel.
My 5th and 6th, a very useful article.
My 4th, 5th and 7th, what Gladstone once was.
My 4th, 1st, 5th and 6th, are very thin.
My 5th, 6th and 7th, what connects England and Ireland.
My 4th, 1st, 5th and 7th, what guides do.
My 7th, 1st, 5th and 4th, what customers do.
My 4th, 5th and 3rd, what loiterers do.
My 2nd, 5th and 3rd, animal.
My 1st, 6th and 7th, the conclusion.
My whole is a word dear to every English heart.

24. **A Charade**

My *first* contains a solid foot
    When used, or when on trial;
Without my *second* not a note
    Can sound on harp or viol;
My *whole*, when in its proper place,
    Within my *first* you'll view;
'Tis strange, but when you've solved the case,
    You'll smile to find it true.

25. Anagrams

The following anagrams represent, when the letters in each case are rearranged, eight different trades or professions. Thus, the letters in the word 'break,' when rearranged, make the word 'baker':

Break. I cut one ear. I start one. It cost bacon. Ladders. Sal or I. Shake more. Sly ware.

26. A Word Square Puzzle

Can you complete the construction of this word square by filling in the missing words? Every word is an English one in common use.

```
N  E  S  T  L  E  S
E     R        T
S     A        E
T  R  A  I  T  O  R
L     T        N
E     O        E
S  T  E  R  N  E  R
```

27. A Charade

My *first* is fair and light as air,
　And often meets our view.
My *next* adorns the rugged thorns
　When wet with pearly dew.
In modest mien my *whole* is seen
　In yonder garden gay;
Its lovely form oft braves the storm
　Of winter's closing day.

28. Buried Poets

In the following lines the names of eight English poets are buried. Can you find them all?

The sun is darting rays of gold
    Upon the moor, enchanting spot;
Whose purpled heights, by Ronald loved,
    Up open to his shepherd cot.
And sundry denizens of air
    Are flying, aye, each to his nest;
And eager make at such an hour
    All haste to reach the mansions blest.

29. Missing Words

I saw her dance like —— upon the green;
    Her gown was white, with —— of yellow dyed;
Her cheeks were like the —— apple seen,
    And now before the —— she stands, a bride.

The four missing words all contain the same six letters.

30. Missing Words

Our parson —— every man who has leisure
    To study —— windows, the glory of fanes;
And —— of devoting his income to pleasure,
    Our —— dean spends his spare money on panes.

The missing words all contain the same seven letters.

31. Decapitations

My whole is in cottage and palace and hall,
And is constantly used by the great and the small.
Beheaded, it still is attached to a head,
And of various colours, black, brown, white, or red.
Behead it again, and all heads would lie low
If deprived of its aid, as you probably know.

32.   **An Enigma**

Five hundred begins, five hundred ends it,

  Five in the middle is seen;

The first of all letters, the first of all figures,

  Take up their stations between.

Join all together, and then you will bring

Before you the name of an eminent king.

33.   **Anagrams**

Rearrange the letters in the following and you may discover twelve different European rivers:

Henri. Le Roi. A gust. O sell me. Set in red. Biter. Sewer. Heron. Sue me. Red pine. Nerves. Maydew.

34.   **A Strange Word**

What English word in common use will describe a person or thing as not to be found in any place whatever, and yet, with no other alteration than a mere space between the syllables, will correctly describe that person or thing as being actually present at this very moment?

35.   **A Charade**

My *first*, for a gift baby utters this sound

My *second's* a weight, and exactly a pound.

My *third*, to reverse, there 'twill quickly be found.

My *whole* is heraldic, resembling a hound.

36.   **A Charade**

My *first* denotes a company,

My *second* shuns a company.

My *third* calls a company,

My *whole* amuses a company.

37. A Cryptic Word

Here is a well-known English word. Can you read it?
E10100010001000UNI100ATXN.

38. The Missing Letters

To each of the following words add two, and the same letters, so as to form a new set of words. The letters may be transposed, but the words must be English ones in use. Christian names are not allowed:

CHAT, PET, RIME, RED, LET, TEA, RAT, CHIP.

39. A Strange Charade

My *first* is a number, my *second* another,

And each, I assure you, will rhyme with the other.

My first, you will find, is one-fifth of my second,

And truly my *whole* a long period reckoned.

Yet my first and my second (nay think not I cozen),

When added together will make but two dozen.

40. Seven Anagrams

1. We all make his praise.
2. Dig over Tom's hill.
3. Will it harm, O hag?
4. John's ready soul.
5. Ha! Meg jogs.
6. Hang joy.
7. Throw sword.

If the letters in the lines are differently arranged, they will spell the names of seven celebrated Englishmen.

41. A Clever Anagram

Can you make one word out of the letters NEW DOOR?

42.   A Sparkling Puzzle

Take the word *sparkling* and cover up or take away one letter so as to leave a new word. Then take away another letter from the new word and leave another word. Continue this, letter by letter, without changing their order, so as to get a new word every time, until you finally leave a word of only one letter.

43.   A Remarkable Plant

Three-quarters of a cross, a circle next,

    Two semicircles then an upright meet;

A triangle upon two legs is set,

    Two semicircles, and a ring complete.

This will give you the name of a well-known plant, greatly appreciated by Thomas Atkins in the trenches.

44.   An Elegant Charade

In my *first* my *second* sat; my *third* and *fourth* I ate.

45.   Word Reversals

Reverse (that is, read backwards) a mechanical power and have a feast. Reverse one who is diseased and have to resist. Reverse an evil one and have resided. Reverse a falsifier and have a banister. Reverse a disposition and have a destiny.

46.   Alphabetical Conundrums

Why is A like noon?

Why is B like a fire?

Why is C like a schoolmistress?

Why is D like a promontory?

Why is E like Death?

Why is F like Paris?

Why is G like plum cake?

Why is H good for deafness?

Why is I the happiest?

Why is J like your nose?

Why is K like a pig's tail?

Why is L like a light?

Why is M a favourite with miners?

Why is N like a pig?

Why is O the only one of the five vowels that you can hear?

Why is P like a man's firstborn?

Why is Q like a guide?

Why is R like Richmond?

Why is S like a furnace in a bullet factory?

Why is T like an island?

Why is U a miserable letter?

Why is V the spoony letter?

Why is W like scandal?

Why does X mean 'to join'?

Why is Y like a pupil?

Why is Z like a cage of monkeys?

47.   **An Arithmetical Charade**

I am a word of five letters. Multiply my *fifth* by two and you have my *first*. Divide my *first* by twenty and you have my *third*. Divide my *third* by five and you have my *second* and *fourth*.

48.   **Missing Words**

In each of the following words three letters, indicated by *'s, are missing, and each missing triplet is the name of an animal. Can you fill them in so that the completed word may make a complete English word?

EDU***ION   BR***RY

PRE***SOR   PY***ID

49.   **Missing Words**

When we were young with —— we played,

And on the jam in —— would raid.

Our lessons though we'd —— with glee,

Upon the —— at games we'd be.

We'd measles, mumps – aye, all the batch;

The —— we now more often catch.

All the missing words contain the same four letters.

50.   **A Charade**

My *second* said, 'I think 'twill be most *whole*

 To go to *first*, where rest and change we'll get.'

I sadly answered, 'I'm not *third*, alas!

 So cannot this *first-second*, I regret.'

51.   **Find the Word**

There is a simple English word of only one syllable that has the peculiarity that if we add one letter at the end it becomes another familiar English word of *three* syllables. Can you find it?

52. A Conundrum

What is it that goes up the hill and down the hill, and yet never moves?

53. Missing Words

Through —— of the sea the tide is making;

   Peaceful and —— is the summer night;

But —— to a voice the stillness breaking:

   ' ——, brave boys, your country bids you fight.'

Better the gold of just and valiant strife

Than the mere —— of a selfish life.

The five missing words contain the same six letters differently arranged.

54. An Enigma

I'm but a little letter, still

Have sacred duties to fulfil;

      But if you take

      My tail, you make

An alteration in my lot;

You'll say I'm shorter–but I'm not.

55. An Enigma

To nothing add ten, with three-fifths of two score,

And let them be joined by five hundred more.

These, rightly conjoined, will give you the name

Of a city that's high in the annals of fame.

56.   A Charade

My *first* a young female has always been reckoned;
And a person of central importance my *second*;
A small preposition my *next* may appear;
And a sign of the Zodiac *brings up the rear.*
These, *united*, are persons who seem much inclined
To do what they can for the good of mankind.

57.   Beheading

Behead a beast, and you will find
A larger beast is left behind.
This is wonderful, you'll say:
A greater wonder I'll display.
Behead this larger beast, and then,
Instead of one, you'll find I'm ten!

58.   Five Anagrams

Can you make five familiar English words by rearranging the letters in each of the following sentences?

'Tis ye govern.
On real catgut.
Made in pint pots.
Into my arm.
There we sat.

59.   An Enigma

There is a well-known word in the English language, the first two letters of which signify a male, the first three a female, the first four a great man, and the whole a great woman.

60. A Charade

My *first* is followed in the chase;
Of men my *next* a numerous race;
My *whole*, alas! if right portrayed,
Will show what's often found in trade.

61. A Transposition

What's that? What's that? Oh, I shall faint.
     Call, call the priest to lay it.
Transpose it, and to king and saint,
     And great and good you pay it.

Both words contain the same letters differently arranged.

62. A Charade

My *first* is a body that's light;
     My *next* a mechanical power.
My *whole* should be found
Where the bottle goes round
     Which enlivens the social hour.

63. Beheading and Curtailing

Complete, I'm a card. Behead me, in brief,
You'll find me a delicate nice bit of beef.
Curtail me, and this time a liquor appears
That raises your spirits and drives away fears.

64. An Enigma

What Spanish instrument's familiar name
And fisher's occupation are the same?

65. An Anagram

If you rightly transpose a false step of the fair,
Just under your nose you'll discover a pair.

66. An Enigma

I am only two letters, but I can wear ten different heads. With one head I am a public notice; with another I am able; with another I am a nickname; with another a lady's indispensable; with another a human being; with another I am an article made of earthenware; with another I am what cowards did from a field of battle; with another I make good leather; with another I am a vehicle; and with another I am pale and sickly. What are the two letters?

67. A Charade

My *first*, when we travel, as useful we deem,
Though drawn, as times alter, with life's changing scheme,
By man, electricity, horses, or steam.

My *second's* a parrot, a dog, or a cat;
But never a hornet, hyena, or bat,
And seldom a mouse or a fox or a rat.

My *whole* a convenience and comfort we call
A luxury, surely, except spring and fall,
When housekeepers make it a trial to all.

68. A Charade

'Mother dear, please say I may
Go down and skate upon the bay.'

'My little son, you cannot go
Upon the ice in the bay below.
This very morn did father say,
Ere to his *whole* he went away,
"John must keep *first* the *second* today."'

69. Curtailment

Astronomers can clearly prove

My whole is ever on the move.

The word curtailed, beyond dispute

A joiner's tool will constitute.

Curtail again, and then, I know,

A form or model you will show.

70. An Anagram

The letters in the following name and address will, if properly rearranged, give the name of a celebrated poet: W. D. Howells, Lawn Forge, Troy, N.H.

71. A Numbered Charade

I am a word of ten letters.

My 1, 2, 8 is rainy.

My 1, 5, 6, 7 is part of a bird's body.

My 8, 9, 10 is a weight.

My 1, 2, 3, 4 is a spring.

My 7, 5, 4, 8 is a golden surface.

My 10, 9, 8, 2 is a short letter.

My whole is a celebrated warrior.

72.   An Enigma

Without a bridle or a saddle,

Across a thing I ride astraddle;

And those I ride, by help of me,

Though almost blind, are made to see.

73.   An Enigma

What is that which goes with a motor lorry, and comes with a motor lorry; is of no use to the motor lorry, and yet the motor lorry cannot move without?

74.   A Charade

My *first* is nothing but a name;

My *second* is more small;

My *whole* is of so little fame,

It has no name at all.

75. An Anagram

Can you make one very familiar word out of the letters contained in the two names CATO, CHLOE?

76. A Charade

Twice name a creature formed for use,
   Man's too much slighted friend;
Myself I next must introduce,
   And with my country end.
My cruel total then appears,
   A stain on history's page,
Sad source of many a mourner's tears,
   In every clime and age.

77. An Enigma

We travel much, yet prisoners are,
   And close confined to boot.
We with the swiftest horse keep pace,
   Yet always go on foot.

78. A Transposition

My whole's a sad catastrophe
   When none to help are nigh it.
Curtail, transpose, and you will see
   Who mostly suffer by it.

79. A Charade

My *first* oft preys upon my *second*;
My *whole* a bitter shrub is reckoned.

80.   An Anagram

Don't lose me, friends, though day and night

I mock the swiftest bird in flight.

I'm murdered by mankind at large.

Reverse me – quickly I discharge.

Transposed, I'm in a bill, 'tis clear.

Once more, an insect will appear.

81.   An Enigma

From a number that's odd cut off the head,

　　It then will even be.

Its tail, I pray, next take away,

　　Your mother then you'll see.

82.   An Anagram

With arrogance swelled, I strut o'er the plain,

And a numerous retinue have in my train.

Transposed, though I now may be horrid and frightful,

Transpose me again, I'm a place most delightful.

83.   A Charade

My *first* to us must point, it's clear,

　　And what I say is true, sir;

My *next* to her your thoughts will steer;

　　My *whole's* an introducer.

84.   A Surprising Relationship

Angelina: 'You say that Mr Tompkins is your uncle?'

Edwin: 'Yes; and I am his uncle.'

Angelina: 'Then – let me see – you must be nephew to each other, of course! Surely you are jesting!'

Edwin: 'Nothing of the kind, I assure you. It is perfect truth. And there has been no breach of the marriage law or disregard of the table of affinity. Funny, isn't it?'

Can you see how this relationship might come about? The explanation is so simple that it can be put into quite a few words. And yet it is so unusual that it will doubtless puzzle the reader.

85.   Lost Property

Porter: 'Lost your luggage, sir? Keep calm, keep calm, and I've no doubt we'll find it somewhere.'

Passenger: 'Ye canna' find it, mon, for it's all through this glass stopper that's come oot.'

Where did this happen?

This is a little puzzle of the 'buried word' class. A town is concealed in the above anecdote.

86.   The City Luncheons

Twelve men connected with a large firm in the City of London sit down to luncheon together every day in the same room. The tables are small ones that only accommodate two persons at the same time. Can you show how these twelve men may lunch together on eleven days in pairs, so that no two of them shall ever sit twice together? We will represent the men by the first twelve letters of the alphabet, and suppose the first day's pairing to be as follows:

(AB) (CD) (EF) (GH) (IJ) (KL).

Then give any pairing you like for the next day, say:

(AC) (BD) (EG) (FH) (IK) (JL),

and so on, until you have completed your eleven lines, with no pair ever occurring twice. There are a good many different arrangements possible. Try to find one of them.

87. The Muddletown Election

At the last Parliamentary election at Muddletown 5,473 votes were polled. The Liberal was elected by a majority of 18 over the Conservative, by 146 over the Independent, and by 575 over the Socialist. Can you give a simple rule for figuring out how many votes were polled for each candidate?

88. That Puzzling Dog

'Something reminds me,' said little Mabel, 'of a little walking puzzle that I recently heard.'

'Let us have it, my dear,' exclaimed Uncle William.

'Well, there is an old lady, Mrs. Smithers, in the next village, who takes a walk every day with her dog.'

'What breed of dog?' asked Reggie.

'Don't be stupid. That doesn't matter a bit. Now, the dog does not run before, behind, or on one side of her. Where does he run?'

'It is clear he must run over her, under her, or inside of her,' said Reggie; but the boy was wrong.

89. The Four Cross-roads

Starting out from a country town to walk to another through quite strange country, I happened to come to a lonely place where four roads met. Some mischievous person had pulled up the signpost and thrown it into the ditch, so that I was completely bewildered as to which road I should take. How did I get out of my difficulty without assistance from any person?

90. Who was First?

Anderson, Biggs and Carpenter were staying together at a place by the seaside. One day they went out in a boat and were a mile at sea when a rifle was fired on shore in their direction. Why or by whom the shot was fired fortunately does not concern us, as no information on these points is obtainable, but from the facts I picked up we can get material for a curious little puzzle for the novice.

It seems that Anderson only heard the report of the gun, Biggs only saw the smoke, and Carpenter merely saw the bullet strike the water near them. Now, the question arises: who first knew of the discharge of the rifle?

91.   Defective Punctuation

A traveller in a little Canadian village spoke to an old man who was sawing wood, and said to him pityingly that he must see few things of interest in so narrow and confined a life. The man replied as follows. Can you, by improved punctuation, bring all his statements into the domain of truth?

Though seldom from my yard I roam,

I saw some strange things here at home.

I saw wood floating in the air;

I saw a skylark, bigger than a bear;

I saw an elephant with arms and hands;

I saw a baby breaking iron bands;

I saw a blacksmith, weighing half a ton;

I saw a statue sing and laugh and run;

I saw a schoolboy nearly ten feet tall;

I saw an oak tree span Niagara fall;

I saw a rainbow, black and white and brown;

I saw a parasol walking through the town;

I saw a politician doing as he should;

I saw a good man – and I saw some wood.

92.   More Punctuation

Here is another little exercise in the art of punctuation. A man wrote this sentence just as it appears, without any stops whatever:

'If is is not is and is not is is what is it is not is and what is it is is not if is not is is?' It will be seen that without punctuation this sentence is meaningless. Can you make sense of it?

93. A Cunning Answer

A facetious individual, who was taking a long walk in the country, came upon a yokel sitting on a stile. He felt convinced that he had dropped on the village idiot, and decided to test the fellow's intelligence by putting to him the simplest question he could think of, which was, 'What day of the week is this, my good man?' The following is the cunning answer that he received:

'When the day after to-morrow is yesterday, to-day will be as far from Sunday as to-day was from Sunday when the day before yesterday was tomorrow.'

Now, what was the day of the week?

94. Freddy's Pudding

Little Freddy said that his helping of pudding was too large. His mamma cut off a piece from it; the helping was still too large. When she had cut from it another piece, it was too small. But, curiously enough, after mamma had cut off from it a third piece, Freddy declared that it was exactly the size he wanted. Can you explain how this could be? It seems contradictory, and would give at first reading the impression that Master Freddy was difficult to please, but a little thought will show that he was quite reasonable in his demands.

95. The Banker and the Note

A banker in a country town was walking down the street when he saw a five-pound note on the kerbstone. He picked it up, noted the number, and went to his private house for luncheon. His wife said that the butcher had sent in his bill for five pounds, and as the only money he had was the note he had found, he gave it to her, and she paid the butcher. The butcher paid it to a farmer in buying a calf, the farmer paid it to a merchant, who in turn paid it to a laundry-woman, and she, remembering that she owed the bank five pounds, went there and paid the note. The banker recognized the note as the one he had found, and by that time it had paid twenty-five pounds' worth of debts. On careful examination he discovered that the note was counterfeit. Now, what was lost in the whole transaction, and by whom?

96. Getting the Wine

A man found a bottle of wine, but he had no corkscrew. How did he extract the wine from the bottle without pulling out the cork, without making a hole in it, and without breaking or piercing the bottle?

97. What are They?

Twice eight are ten of us, and ten but three;
Three of us are five. What can we be?
If this be not enough, I'll tell you more –
Twelve of us are six, and nine but four.

98. Strange, though True

There is a certain district in Sussex where any sound and well-proportioned horse may travel, quite regularly, thirty miles per day, yet while its off legs are going this distance its near legs will unavoidably pass over nearly thirty-one miles. It would at first appear that the near legs of the creature must be nearly a mile ahead of the horse at the end of the journey, but the animal does not seem to mind, for, as a matter of fact, he finishes his task quite whole and sound. Can you explain?

99.   A Historical Puzzle

The following lines were written by Arthur Connor, a prominent figure in the Irish Rebellion of 1798. He was arrested, and wrote the verses while in prison. He made his escape to France in 1807, where he became a general in the army and died aged eighty-seven.

> The pomps of Courts and pride of kings
>
> I prize above all earthly things;
>
> I love my country, but the King,
>
> Above all men, his praise I sing.
>
> The Royal banners are displayed,
>
> And may success the standard aid.

> I fain would banish far from hence
>
> The 'Rights of Man' and 'Common Sense.'
>
> Confusion to his odious reign,
>
> That foe to princes, Thomas Paine.
>
> Defeat and ruin seize the cause
>
> Of France, its liberties and laws.

These two apparently loyal verses, if properly read, bear a very different meaning. Can you discover it?

100.   Strange Arithmetic

'From half of five take one and let five remain.' Can you do this?

101. Some Maxims

The following represents five old maxims, and the puzzle is to read them correctly:

Never	All	For he who	Everything	Often	More than
Tell	You may know	Tells	He knows	Tells	He knows
Attempt	You can do	Attempts	He can do	Attempts	He can do
Believe	You may hear	Believes	He hears	Believes	He hears
Lay out	You can afford	Lays out	He can afford	Lays out	He can afford
Decide upon	You may see	Decides upon	He sees	Decides upon	He sees

102. The Three Tea-cups

Can you place ten lumps of sugar in three tea-cups so that there shall be an odd number of lumps in every cup? Do not give it up as impossible, because it can certainly be done.

103. The Handcuffed Spies

Nine spies were captured somewhere in France, and as they were of a particularly dangerous character, they had to be carefully guarded while waiting their trial. Every weekday they were taken out for exercise, handcuffed together, as shown in the sketch made by a correspondent on the spot. On no day in any one week were the same two men to be handcuffed together. It will be seen how they were sent out on Monday. Can you arrange the nine men in triplets for the remaining five days? It will be seen that No. 1 cannot be again handcuffed to No. 2 (on either side), nor No. 2 with No. 3; but, of course, No. 1 and No. 3 can be put together.

104. The Lost Battle

An old general was discussing a serious reverse and deploring his heavy losses. The actual state of things is recorded in the following lines:

> To his dismay
> He learned next day
> What havoc war had wrought;
> He had at most
> But half his host,
> Plus ten times three, six, nought.
> One-eighth were lain
> On beds of pain,
> With hundreds six beside;
> One-fifth were dead,
> Captives or fled,
> Last in grim warfare's tide.

Can you, from these facts, say just how many men the general had in his army before he engaged in battle?

105. A Strange Sentence

Can you read the following sentence?

OPM & BR FMNAC & TRR R UUULE NMEE 2 NRG & O 2 B ODS 2 U DR LN.

106. Another Strange Sentence

Can you read the following sentence?

O MLE B9 & FMN8 B4 U X10U8 NE XS UU AYY 11 SS1010.

107. A Riddle

I am a word of five letters. My *first* minus my *fifth* will leave my *second*; my fifth divided by my first will produce my *fourth*; and five times my first added to five times my fifth will make my *third*; my *whole* is funny.

108. A Charade

My *first* is a short sleep. My *second* is a relation. My *whole* is an article in daily use.

109. Another Charade

My *first* is a part of the human face. My *second* is an unpleasant sensation. My *third* is an article. My whole is a small animal.

110. Enigmatic Names of Birds

The following descriptions give enigmatic clues for birds. For example, 'a tall bird going through a doorway' could be a *duck*, since it would have to 'duck' to go through the doorway.

a) The bird that was in Eden.

b) The bird that is easily cheated.

c) A chess-man.

d) A letter.

e) An architect.

f) A country in Europe.

g) The bird that's full of mischief and fun.

h) The bird that raises great weights.

i) The bird that is part of a fence.

j) The bird that is always in fear.

k) The bird that assists at your meals.

l) The bird that's a plaything for children.

111. Enigmatic Names of Beverages

a) A sailor's desire.

b) Counterfeit agony.

c) An island in the Atlantic.

d) Ghosts.

e) A letter.

112. Enigmatic Names of Plants

a) A fop, and an animal.

b) A period of time and a US consonant.

c) A blackbird and its claw.

d) Sunrise.

e) A pronoun.

f) A part of the head of a farm animal.

113. A Riddle

My first is found in every house,

From wintry winds it guards.

My second is the highest found – in every pack of cards.

My whole, a Scottish chief, is praised

By ballad, bard, and story,

Who for his country gave his life,

And, dying, fell with glory.

114. A Conundrum

My first is a part of the day,

My last a conductor of light,

My whole to take measure of time,

Is useful by day and by night.

115. A Charade

I'm in the book, but not on any leaf;

I'm in the mouth, but not in lip or teeth;

I'm in the atmosphere, but never in the air;

I wait on every one, but never on a pair;

I am with you wherever you may go;

And every thing you do I'm sure to know;

Though when you did it I should not be there,

Yet when 'twas done, you'd find me in the chair.

116. A Charade

My first is an instrument, which, though small, has more power than any monarch on earth. It is the lover's friend and the poet's pride; yet has overthrown kingdoms, ruined reputations, set folks together by the ears, and caused more destruction than plagues, pestilence, or famine. My second, though not quite so mischievous, is very destructive when in improper hands, and my whole, though employed against my first, is deemed its friend and improver.

117. Beheading and Transposing

I'm composed of letters four,

A turkey, cock, or hen;

Behead me, and I upward soar.

Put on my head again,

Transpose me, then a beast I am,

Both bloodthirsty and wild,

That preys on many a helpless lamb,

And oft devours a child.

118. A Charade

I have wings, yet never fly—
I have sails, yet never go—
I can't keep still, if I try,
Yet forever stand just so.

119. A Transposition

I am a word of four letters often used in prayer.

Transposed, I become what every one professes.

Transposed again, I become an adjective, the qualities of which everyone despises.

Transposed again, I am part of a horse.

120. A Charade

In every hedge my *second* is,
As well as every tree,
And when poor school-boys act amiss,
It often is their fee.
My *first* likewise is always wicked,
Yet ne'er committed sin,
My *total* for my first is fitted,
Composed of brass or tin.

121. The Traveller's Puzzle

The puzzle in this case is to place the point of your pencil on one of the blanks and strike out every letter once until you come back to the other blank, without lifting your pencil. If you do this in the fewest possible straight lines, the letters at the turning points ought to spell out the name of a book. What is the name of that book?

N	E	O	L	O	G	I	C
A	B	L	U	T	I	O	N
D	I	A	M	O	N	D	S
O	B	V	E	R	S	E	S
	S	U	N	B	U	R	N
	P	U	Z	Z	L	E	R
S	O	L	U	T	I	O	N
U	P	H	O	L	D	E	R

Chapter 6. Modern Puzzles

This chapter consists of contemporary puzzles created for the World Puzzle Federation's yearly Puzzle Grand Prix event.

1.   Battleships

Locate the indicated fleet in the grid. Each piece of a ship occupies a single cell. A cell that does not contain a ship piece is considered 'sea'. Ships can be rotated. Ships do not touch each other, not even diagonally (that is, if two ship pieces are in adjacent cells, they must be part of the same ship). The contents of some cells are given for you.

Each number to the right and bottom of the grid reveals the number of ship pieces that must be located in that row or column (including any that might be given for you).

a)

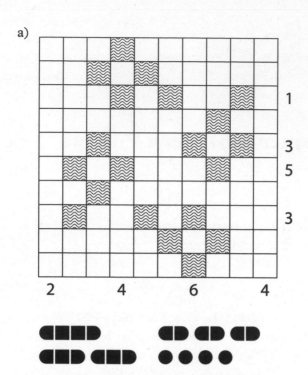

b)

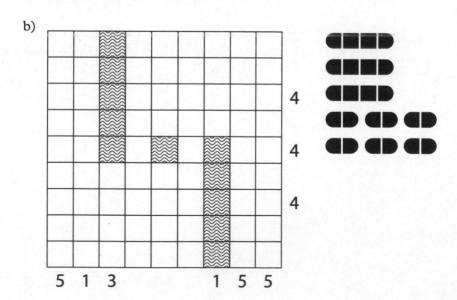

2. Elastic Bands

Fill in each circle with a letter so that the two networks are identical; that is, if two letters have a line connecting them in one network, then those two letters have a line connecting them in the other network, and vice versa.

Example solution:

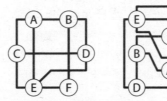

a)

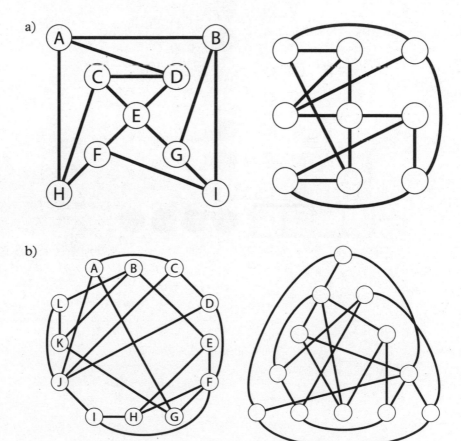

b)

3.   **Mastermind**

Each row represents a guess at a secret code. A black dot represents a letter in the guess that is in the same position as a letter in the secret code. A white dot represents a letter in the guess that is in the secret code, but not in the same position. The dots are given in no specific order, and each letter in the secret code contributes at most one dot with black dots given priority over white dots in case of ambiguity (for example, if the guess was FREED and the codeword was GEESE, the puzzle would display 1 black and 1 white). Each letter in the secret code appears in at least one guess. Blank spaces can appear in the guesses but will never appear in the secret code.

The secret code may or may not be a word.

a)

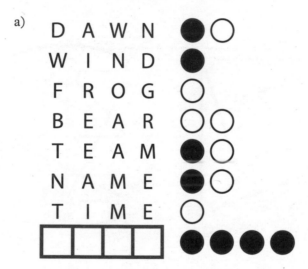

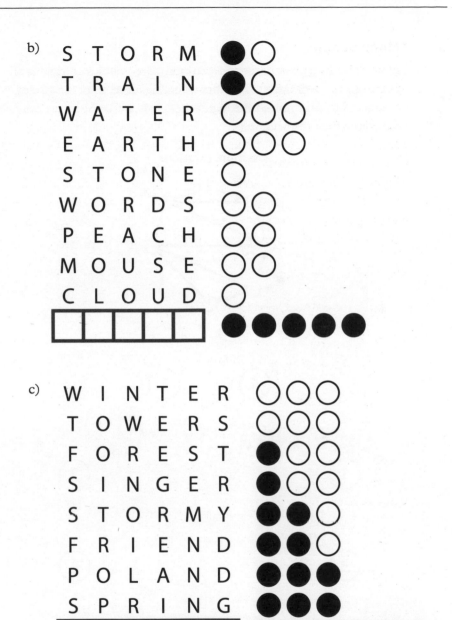

4.   **Connections**

Draw straight connections between numbered circles so that each
circle has the appropriate number of connections to other circles.
Connections may not go through other circles. Connections may not
intersect other connections.

Example solution:

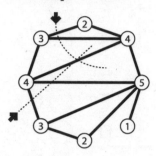

a)

b)

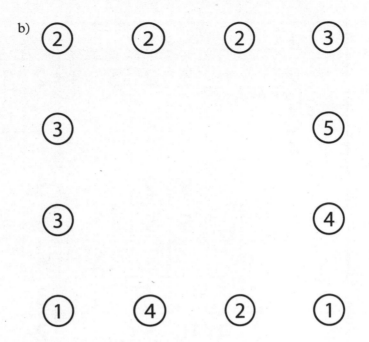

5. Fillomino

Divide the grid along the dotted lines into regions (called polyominoes) so that no two polyominoes with the same area share an edge. Inside some cells are numbers; each number must equal the area of the polyomino it belongs to. A polyomino may contain zero, one, or more of the given numbers. (It is possible to have a 'hidden' polyomino: a polyomino without any of the given numbers. 'Hidden' polyominoes may have any area, including a value not present in the starting grid, such as a 6 in a puzzle with only clues numbered 1–5.)

Example solution:

a)

	1								
	2			3	3	5	3	2	1
	3								
	4								
	5			5	2			5	
	6			5	5			5	
								4	
								3	
3	1	2	4	10	5			2	
								1	

b)

	2	7	3			5	1	5	
	7		2			1		7	
	3	2	1			6	5	7	
				3	6				
				6	3				
	1	2	4			6	5	2	
	6		6			5		5	
	4	6	4			5	5	2	

6. Minesweeper

Place mines into the unnumbered cells in the grid, at most one mine per cell, so that each number in a cell represents the number of mines adjacent to that cell (including diagonally adjacent cells).

Example solution:

0		3	●
		●	●
3	●	4	
●	●		

a)

5		3	4	4	3		6	
4			2	2			5	
4		2			2		2	
2		2			2		2	
2			2	2			1	
2		4	2	4	5		6	

b)

									2
	6	5	5	6	6	4	4		
								4	
	4	3	4	3			5		
3					4		4		
4		2					4		
3			2	4	4	4			
4									
	3	4	3	4	3	3	4		
2									

7.   Graffiti

Blacken some cells in the grid and draw a closed loop through all
other cells in the grid. The loop connects the centres of cells
orthogonally, and never goes through a cell more than once. Some
rows have number clues next to them. The numbers represent, in left-
to-right order, the exact size of groups of consecutive black cells in
those rows. Groups are separated by at least one non-blackened cell.
As a special case, if the clue '0' is given, it means there are no
blackened cells in that row. Similar clues may be given for some
columns (using top-to-bottom order).

Example solution:

a)

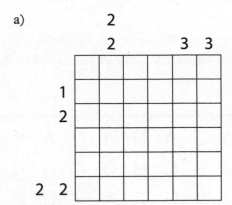

b)

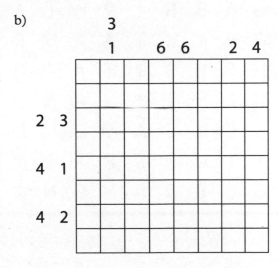

8.   Word Search

Locate the list of words in the grid. Words always appear in a line in one of the eight standard directions. The leftover letters will spell out a further country.

```
S  O  R  O  M  O  C  A  N  A  D  A  E
O  C  H  A  D  U  B  O  H  Q  C  G  K
A  G  L  Q  B  H  B  H  A  A  Y  U  Y
L  I  O  A  U  A  B  R  I  P  W  L  A
B  E  R  T  G  A  I  B  T  A  A  M  R
A  R  A  A  H  E  R  B  I  T  A  I  R
N  N  A  R  G  E  N  T  I  N  A  N  O
I  A  A  Z  S  L  A  E  A  M  D  M  D
A  I  R  H  I  I  U  P  S  P  A  I  N
N  M  U  I  G  L  E  B  A  N  O  N  A
```

ALBANIA	INDIA
ANDORRA	IRAN
ARGENTINA	IRAQ
BAHRAIN	ISRAEL
BELGIUM	ITALY
BHUTAN	KUWAIT
BRAZIL	LAOS
BULGARIA	LEBANON
CANADA	MALI
CHAD	NAMIBIA
COMOROS	OMAN
CUBA	PANAMA
EGYPT	QATAR
GABON	SENEGAL
GHANA	SERBIA
HAITI	SPAIN
	TOGO

9. Bent Word Search

Locate the list of words in the grid. Words always appear in a bent line; they start in one of the eight standard directions, bend at right angles at exactly one letter (that is not the first or last letter), and continue in the new direction.

Two words will not be found in the grid.

Example solution:

ALBA
BAGGAGE
BANAL
BANG
GALA
LAB

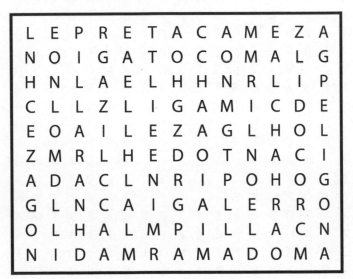

ALLIGATOR
ARMADILLO
CAMEL
CATERPILLAR
CHINCHILLA
CROCODILE
GAZELLE
GORILLA
LION
LLAMA
MANDRILL
PELICAN

10. Word Search

Locate the list of words in the grid. Words always appear in a line in one of the eight standard directions. Some letters in the middle of the grid (inside the dotted lines) are missing and you must rediscover what they are while solving.

One word will not be found in the grid.

Example solution:

GLAD
SAD
SLAB
BAD
DRAB

```
B E N E C M C B U M V I S T A M F K O
U S T A O R I E N A J E D O I R H R B
P K L H E G R E K P N B Q K C W S A I
A O R P R O W R F A B S U D F I N L E
C P I V I Y S D T J O T I M O G E J H
H R W A O G N T E N R E N N A B N E A
E I O R N A X H A G A V S L N I C V W
S V K I R A S         O J J O E I M
T N J C N E B         A C S P L C P
L I M D E L K         N B T A Z A G
B C H K S N O         R U O T C N A
O A O P O R E         T D R I I P N
P Y I D D T L S N K O F W A E J L M A
A S N N M U V G A B L V L P I A R Y S
Z O X A O E P I N N O I D E Y D A O T
L O H I Y S H A W A C T B S G M L R A
M E B N O M R N L U B N A T S I J K M
Q U S E I E Z E R V S R I M P L E B A
L D O R P N I G L A X M H K A C D L O
```

NEWYORK   STAMFORD   ANTALYA
BRNO   OULU   PAPROTNIA
COLOGNE   ARNHEM   KRALJEVICA
POIANABRASOV   OPATIJA   BEIJING
UTRECHT   EGER   LONDON
KOPRIVNICA   BOROVETS   SOFIA
ISTANBUL   RIODEJANEIRO   SENEC
BUDAPEST   MINSK   BANGALORE

11.   Password Path

Find a path that starts in the upper-left letter and ends in the lower-right letter, that goes through each letter once and repeats only the password (given below the grid). The path may only travel in the eight standard directions and may *not* intersect itself.

Example solution:

PUZZLE

a)

D	O	D	O
D	D	O	D
O	D	O	D
O	D	O	O

DO

b)

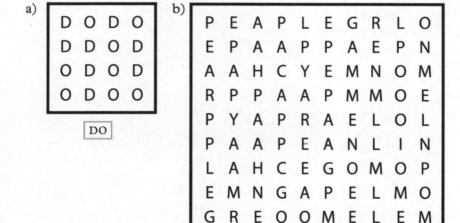

PEACHPEARPAPAYAAPPLEGRAPEMANGOLEMONMELONPOMELOLIME

12. Alphabet Blocks

There are multiple cubes, each of which has six faces. Each face is labelled with a letter. No letter appears more than once. For each of the words in the list, it is possible to spell the word using all the cubes, one cube for each letter in the word. Determine which letters are on which cube. Ignore rotations of the letters (for example, you may not use the same face for 'M' and 'W').

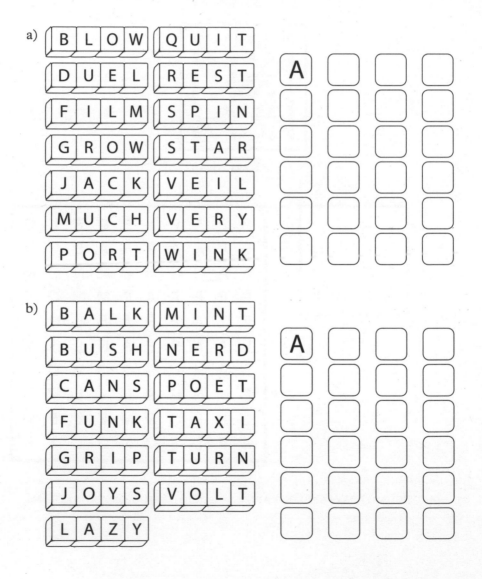

13. Build a Criss-cross

Place the pieces to form a crisscross pattern. Cells that touch on an edge must be part of the same word. Each word reads left-to-right or top-to-bottom, and fits the provided category. The list of words is not given, but a lined grid is.

Example solution:

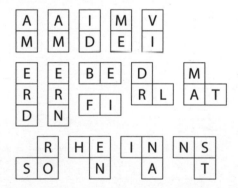

a) Category: Capitals

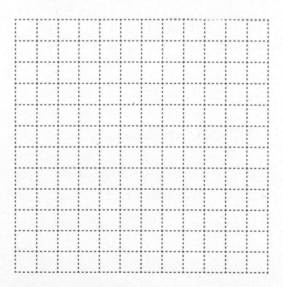

b) Category: In Orbit

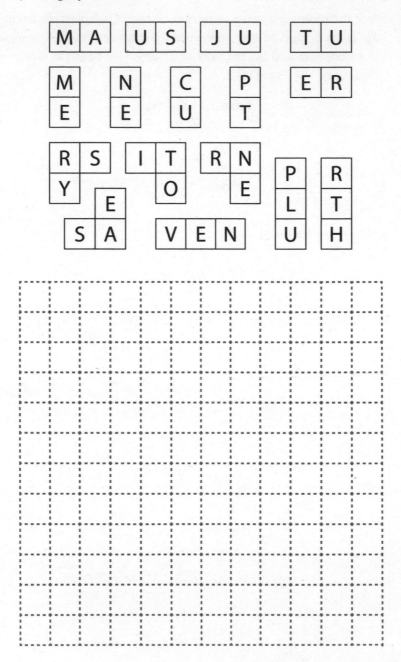

14.   **Mini Quiz**

Select an answer for each question such that the answers are correct and consistent.

a)

Q1.	Q2.	Q3.
How many times is 'A' chosen in this quiz?	How many times is 'B' chosen in this quiz?	How many times is 'C' chosen in this quiz?

Q1.	Q2.	Q3.
A. 0	A. 0	A. 0
B. 1	B. 2	B. 1
C. 2	C. 1	C. 2

b)

Q1.	Q2.	Q3.	Q4.	Q5.
Answer of Q2 minus answer of Q3 equals	Answer of Q3 minus answer of Q4 equals	Answer of Q5 plus answer of Q4 equals	Product of answers for Q1, Q2 and Q3 is	Sum of all answers in this quiz equals

Q1.	Q2.	Q3.	Q4.	Q5.
A. −1	A. −2	A. −1	A. −2	A. −1
B. 1	B. −1	B. 1	B. −1	B. 1
C. 2	C. 1	C. 2	C. 1	C. 2

c)

Q1.	Q2.	Q3.	Q4.	Q5.
Are the answers for Q2 and Q3 the same?	Are the answers for Q1 and Q2 the same?	Are the answers for Q2 and Q4 the same?	Are the answers for Q1 and Q2 different?	Are the answers for Q1 and Q3 the same?

Q1.	Q2.	Q3.	Q4.	Q5.
A. yes	A. yes	A. yes	A. yes	A. yes
B. no	B. no	B. no	B. no	B. no

15.   Scrabble

Put at most one letter into each cell so that the given words can be read either across (left-to-right) or down (top-to-bottom) in consecutive cells in the grid. Every word must appear in the grid exactly once, and no other words may appear in the grid (that is, if two cells are filled and are adjacent, then there must be a word that uses both of them). Every word must have either a blank cell or the edge of the grid before and after it. All letters must be (orthogonally) connected in a single group.

The starting cell of each word is marked with a circle.

Example solution:

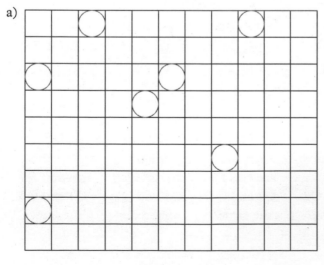

a)

INDIA
SLOVAKIA
GERMANY
HUNGARY
USA
SERBIA
NETHERLANDS
RUSSIA

b)

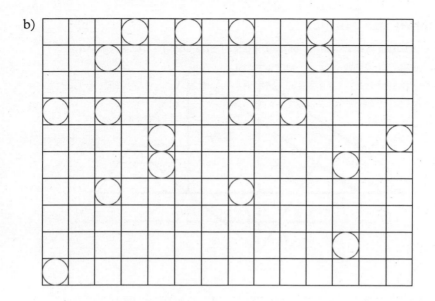

ALL	IN
GREAT	SINGLE
THINGS	WORDS
ARE	FREEDOM
SIMPLE	JUSTICE
AND	HONOR
MANY	DUTY
CAN	MERCY
BE	HOPE
EXPRESSED	

16.   Count the Shapes

Determine the number of triangles of any size in the diagram.

a)

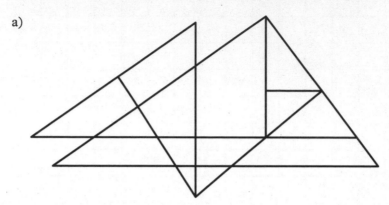

Determine the number of rectangles of any size in the diagram.

b)

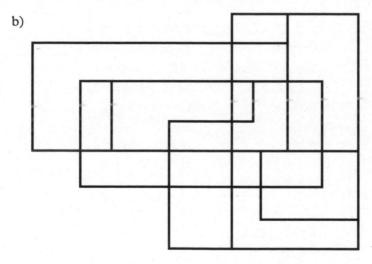

17.   Pyramid Climbers

Each cell at the bottom of the pyramid has a 'climber' associated with it. Each climber climbs up a path of adjacent cells, each containing a different letter. (Climbers do not climb sideways.) Each cell is reached by exactly one climber.

Example solution:

a)

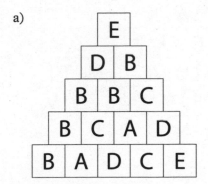

b)

c)

18. Common Letters

Put each word into a different box such that the number between two boxes indicates the number of letters those words have in common. Duplicate letters are counted separately; for example, AABBB and BBCCA have three letters in common.

Example solution:

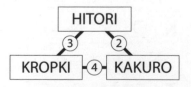

a)

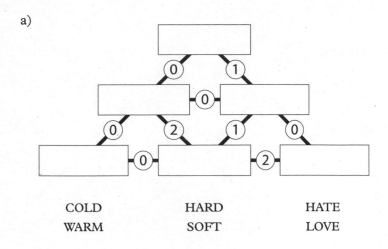

COLD   HARD   HATE
WARM   SOFT   LOVE

b)

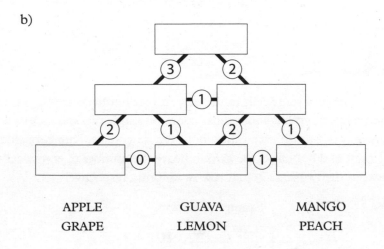

APPLE   GUAVA   MANGO
GRAPE   LEMON   PEACH

c)

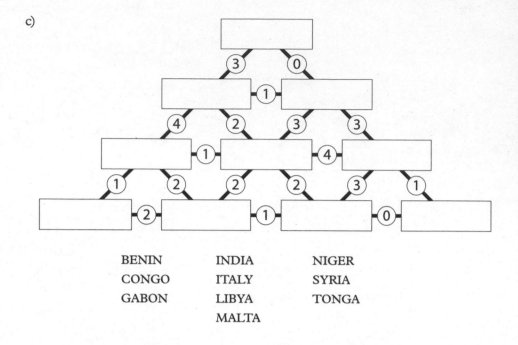

BENIN	INDIA	NIGER
CONGO	ITALY	SYRIA
GABON	LIBYA	TONGA
	MALTA	

19. Star Gaps

Place stars into some cells in the grid, no more than one star per cell. Each row and each column must contain exactly two stars. Cells with stars may not touch each other, not even diagonally. Numbers along the right and bottom of the grid indicate the number of empty cells between the two stars in that row or column, respectively.

Example solution:

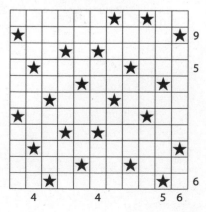

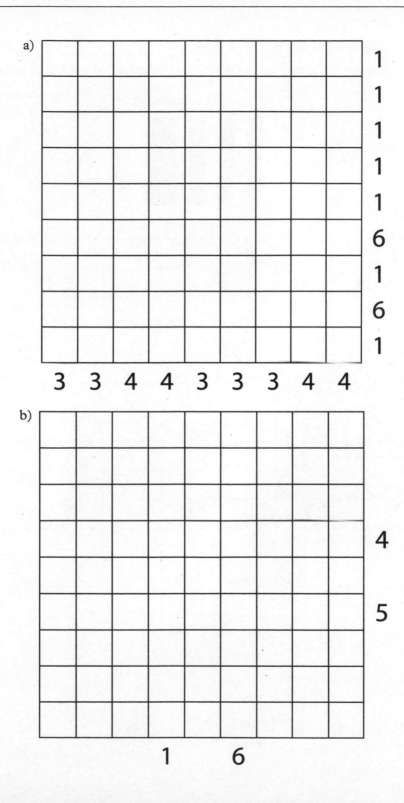

20. Column Dance

Remove some columns so that there is exactly one symbol in each row.

Example solution:

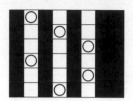

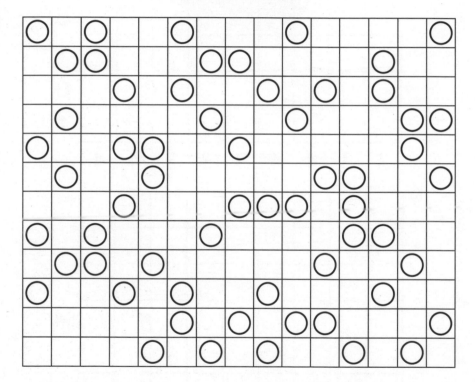

21. Arithmetic Square

Place each number from 1 to 9 into the cells (a different single number in each cell) so that the indicated equations/relations are correct. Evaluate from left-to-right and top-to-bottom (ignore the usual precedence of the operators).

It is possible for expressions and partial expressions to be negative or non-integral.

Example solution:

$$
\begin{array}{ccccccc}
\boxed{9} & + & \boxed{8} & + & \boxed{7} & > 23 \\
+ & & - & & + \\
\boxed{6} & \times & \boxed{4} & \div & \boxed{3} & = 8 \\
\times & & \times & & - \\
\boxed{5} & \times & \boxed{2} & + & \boxed{1} & = 11 \\
= & & = & & = \\
75 & & 8 & & 9
\end{array}
$$

a)

$$
\begin{array}{ccccccc}
\boxed{} & \times & \boxed{} & - & \boxed{} & = 10 \\
\times & & - & & + \\
\boxed{} & - & \boxed{} & - & \boxed{} & = 0 \\
- & & - & & + \\
\boxed{} & - & \boxed{} & + & \boxed{} & = 12 \\
= & & = & & = \\
10 & & 0 & & 12
\end{array}
$$

b)

$$\square \div \square \times \square = 2$$
$$\div \qquad \times \qquad -$$
$$\square \times \square - \square = 1$$
$$\times \qquad - \qquad +$$
$$\square + \square - \square = 4$$
$$= \qquad = \qquad =$$
$$2 \qquad 1 \qquad 8$$

c)

$$\square \times \square \times \square < 83$$
$$+ \qquad + \qquad +$$
$$\square \times \square \times \square < 74$$
$$+ \qquad + \qquad +$$
$$\square \times \square \times \square < 65$$
$$> \qquad > \qquad >$$
$$13 \qquad 14 \qquad 15$$

22.   **Arukone**

Some cells in the grid are marked with numbers; each number appears exactly twice and no cell contains more than one number. For each pair of identical numbers, draw a path that connects those two numbers. The paths must go through orthogonally adjacent cells. Each cell may be visited by at most one path, and may be visited at most once by that path. (It is permissible for a cell to not be visited by any path.)

Example solution:

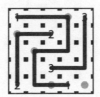

a)

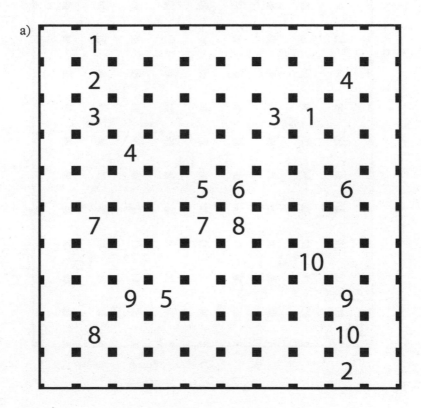

b)

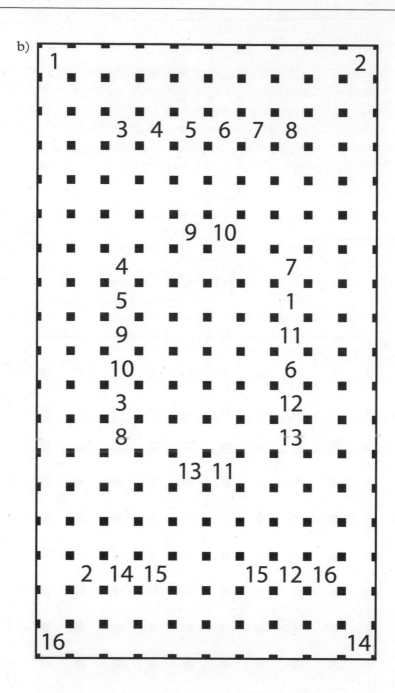

c)

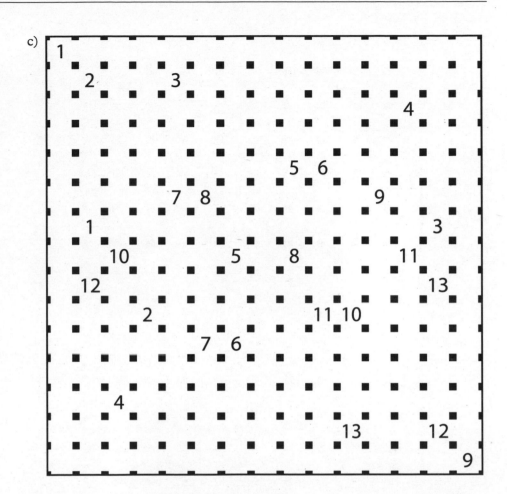

Solutions

Solutions: Chapter 1.
Early Puzzles

1.   A Sumerian Riddle

A school.

2.   Cleobulus' 'Year Riddle'

The father is a year, his children months, and his grandchildren days (white) and nights (black).

3.   The Riddle of the Sphinx

Man: he crawls as a child, walks upright in his prime and uses a cane in his old age.

4.   Symphosius

a) A mother of twins.

b) A mule.

5.   Aldhelm

a) A dog.

b) A woman in labour with twins.

6.   **Claret**

An eye. (The puzzle is deliberately written to mislead you!)

7.   **Samuel Danforth**

Ships.

8.   **From** *The Merry Book of Riddles*

A thorn (which got caught in the man's foot).

9.   **Jonathan Swift**

A fan.

10.   **George Canning**

Cares (and caress).

11.   **A Musician's Riddle**

Henry Purcell.

12.   **Voltaire**

Time.

13.   **From Horatio Walpole's** *Works*

Today.

14.   **From** *The Penny Post*

Maidstone.

15.   **From** *The Gentleman and Lady's Town and Country Magazine*

The answers to each line in order are: Bed, Oh, Sin, Tobacco, Oak and Noun. The initials of these answers in order spell out BOSTON.

16. **From *The Little Puzzling Cap***

A pair of scissors.

17. **Catherine Fanshawe**

The letter 'h'.

18. **From 'The Enigmas' column in *The Minerva***

Justice.

19. **From *Farmer's Almanack***

Nothing.

Solutions: Chapter 2. Mathematical Puzzles

1.   Concerning a Cheque

If you set to work under the notion that there were only pounds and shillings – no pence – in the amount, a solution is impossible. The amount must have been £5 11s. 6d. He received £11 5s. 6d., and after he had spent half a crown there would remain the sum of £11 3s., which is twice the amount of the cheque.

2.   Pocket-money

The amount originally in pocket was £19 18s., so that after spending one-half I had remaining £9 19s., or as many shillings as previously pounds and half as many pounds as shillings.

3.   Dollars and Cents

The man must have entered the store with $99.98 in his pocket.

4.   Loose Cash

The largest sum is 15s. 9d., composed of a crown and a half-crown (or three half-crowns), four florins and a threepenny-piece.

5.   Doubling the Value

The only answer is £2 17s. multiplied by six, which will produce £17 2s., where the pounds change places with the shillings as required.

6.   Generous Gifts

At first there were twenty persons, and each received 6s. Then fifteen persons (five fewer) would have received 8s. each. But twenty-four (four more) appeared and only received 5s. each. The amount distributed weekly was thus 120s.

7.   Selling Eggs

The smallest possible number of eggs is 103, and the woman sold 60 every day. Any multiple of these two numbers will work. Thus, she might have started with 206 eggs and sold 120 daily; or with 309 and sold 180 daily. But we required the smallest possible number.

8.   Buying Buns

There must have been three boys and three girls, each of whom received two buns at three a penny and one bun at two a penny, the cost of which would be exactly sevenpence.

9.   Unrewarded Labour

Weary Willie must have worked $16\frac{2}{3}$ days and idled $13\frac{1}{3}$ days. Thus the former time, at 8s. a day, amounts to exactly the same as the latter at 10s. a day, that is £6 13s. 4d.

10.   The Perplexed Banker

The contents of the ten bags should be as follows: 1, 2, 4, 8, 16, 32, 64, 128, 256, 489. The first nine numbers are in geometrical progression, and their sum, deducted from 1000, gives the contents of the tenth bag.

11.   A Weird Game

The seven men, A, B, C, D, E, F and G, had respectively in their
pockets before play the following sums, reduced to farthings for the
sake of simplicity: 449, 225, 113, 57, 29, 15 and 8. The answer may
be found by laboriously working backwards, but a simpler method is
as follows: 7+1=8; 2×7+1=15; 4×7+1=29; and so on, where the
multiplier increases in powers of 2, that is, 2, 4, 8, 16, 32 and 64.

12.   Find the Coins

Abel had at first 16s. 3d., Best had 8s. 9d., and Crewe had 5s. Abel
and Best must each have had a threepenny-piece, but as there must
have been an even number of these pieces, divisible by three, the
fewest possible threepenny-pieces is six. Then the 8s. 9d. first paid to
B. in the fewest possible coins would be 5s., 2s. 6d., 1s., and 3d. – four
coins – the 5s. paid to C. would be a crown, and the 2s. 6d. left with A.
would be a half-crown. If A. thus had the minimum of six coins, B.
had seven coins and C. five coins, and each had six coins at the finish.
In short, A. started with 2 crowns, 2 half-crowns, a shilling and a
threepenny-piece, B. with a crown, 3 shillings and 3 threepenny-
pieces, and C. with a half-crown, 2 shillings and 2 threepenny-pieces.
The reader will now have no difficulty in making the various payments
so that each man is left with 1 crown, 1 half-crown, 2 shillings and 2
threepenny-pieces.

13.   An Easy Settlement

At the start of play Andrews held a half-sovereign and a shilling, Baker
held a crown and a florin, and Carey held a double florin and a half-
crown. After settlement, Andrews held double florin and florin, Baker
the half-sovereign and half-crown, and Carey held crown and shilling.
Thus, Andrews lost 5s., Carey lost 6d., and Baker won 5s. 6d. The
selection of the coins is obvious, but their allotment requires a little
judgment and trial.

14.   Digging a Ditch

A. should receive one-third of two pounds (13s. 4d.), and B. two-
thirds (£1 6s. 8d.). Say B. can dig all in 2 hours and shovel all in 4
hours; then A. can dig all in 4 hours and shovel all in 8 hours. That is,

their ratio of digging is as 2 to 4 and their ratio of shovelling as 4 to 8 (the same ratio), and A. can dig in the same time that B. can shovel (4 hours), while B. can dig in a quarter of the time that A. can shovel. Any other figures will do that fill these conditions and give two similar ratios for their working ability. Therefore, A. takes one-third and B. twice as much – two-thirds.

15.   Name their Wives

As it is evident that Catherine, Jane, and Mary received respectively £122, £132 and £142, making together the £396 left to the three wives, if John Smith receives as much as his wife Catherine, £122; Henry Snooks half as much again as his wife Jane, £198; and Tom Crowe twice as much as his wife Mary, £284, we have correctly paired these married couples and exactly accounted for the £1000.

16.   Market Transactions

The man bought 19 cows for £95, 1 sheep for £1, and 80 rabbits for £4, making together 100 animals at a cost of £100.

A purely arithmetical solution is not difficult by a method of averages, the average cost per animal being the same as the cost of a sheep.

By algebra we proceed as follows, working in shillings:

$$100x + 20y + z = 2000$$
$$x + y + z = 100$$
$$\overline{99x + 19y = 1900}$$

by subtraction. We have therefore to solve this indeterminate equation, when we find that the only answer is $x=19$, $y=1$. Then, to make up the 100 animals, z must $=80$.

17.   Their Ages

Tom's age was seven years and Mary's thirteen years.

18.   Mrs Wilson's Family

The ages must have been as follows: Mrs Wilson, 39; Edgar, 21; James, 18; John, 18; Ethel, 12; Daisy, 9. It is clear that James and John were twins.

19.   De Morgan and Another

De Morgan was born in 1806. When he was 43, the year was the square of his age – 1849. Jenkins was born in 1860. He was 5^2+6^2 (61) in the year 5^4+6^4 (1921). Also he was 2×31 (62) in the year 2×31^2 (1922). Again, he was 3×5 (15) in the year 3×5^4 (1875).

20.   'Simple' Arithmetic

Their ages were respectively 64 and 20.

21.   A Dreamland Clock

The hour indicated would be exactly $23\frac{1}{13}$ minutes after 4 o'clock. But as the minute-hand moved in the opposite direction, the real time would be $36\frac{12}{13}$ minutes after 4. You must deduct the number of minutes indicated from 60 to get the real time.

22.   What is the Time?

The time is $6\frac{3}{4}$ minutes past IX, when the hour-hand is $45\frac{9}{16}$ minutes past XII. Then $45\frac{9}{16}$ is the square of $6\frac{3}{4}$. If we allow fractions *less* than a minute point then there is also the solution, five seconds (one-twelfth of a minute) past XII o'clock.

23.   Hill Climbing

It must have been $6\frac{3}{4}$ miles to the top of the hill. He would go up in $4\frac{1}{2}$ hours and descend in $1\frac{1}{2}$ hours.

24.   Timing the Motor-car

As the man can walk 27 steps while the car goes 162, the car is clearly going six times as fast as the man. The man walks $3\frac{1}{2}$ miles an hour: therefore the car was going at 21 miles an hour.

25.   The Staircase Race

If the staircase were such that each man would reach the top in a certain number of full leaps, without taking a reduced number at his last leap, the smallest possible number of risers would, of course, be 60 (that is, 3×4×5). But the sketch showed us that A. taking three risers at a leap, has one odd step at the end; B. taking four at a leap, will have three only at the end; and C. taking five at a leap, will have four only at the finish. Therefore, we have to find the smallest number that, when divided by 3, leaves a remainder 1, when divided by 4 leaves 3, and when divided by 5 leaves a remainder 4. This number is 19. So there were 19 risers in all, only four being left out in the sketch.

26.   A Walking Puzzle

It will be found (and it is the key to the solution) that the man from B. can walk 7 miles while the man from A. can walk 5 miles. Say the distance between the towns is 24 miles, then the point of meeting would be 14 miles from A. and the man from A. walked $3\frac{3}{7}$ miles per hour, while the man from B. walked $4\frac{4}{5}$ miles per hour. They both arrived at 7 p.m. exactly.

27.   Riding in the Wind

He could ride one mile in $3\frac{3}{7}$ minutes, or $\frac{7}{24}$ mile per minute. The wind would help or retard him to the extent of $\frac{1}{24}$ mile per minute. Therefore, with the wind he could ride $\frac{8}{24}$ mile per minute and against the wind $\frac{6}{24}$ mile per minute; so that is 1 mile in 3 minutes, or 4 minutes respectively, as stated.

28.   A Rowing Puzzle

The correct answer is $3\frac{9}{17}$ minutes. The crew can row $\frac{1}{5}$ of the distance per minute on still water, and the stream does $\frac{1}{12}$ of the distance per minute. The difference and sum of these two fractions are $\frac{7}{60}$ and $\frac{17}{60}$. Therefore, against the stream would take $\frac{60}{7}$ minutes (or $8\frac{4}{7}$ minutes), and with the stream $\frac{60}{17}$ (or $3\frac{9}{17}$ minutes).

29. The Moving Stairway

If I walk 26 steps I require 30 seconds, and if I walk 34 steps I require only 18 seconds. Multiply 30 by 34 and 26 by 18 and we get 1020 and 468, the difference between which is 552. Divide this by the difference between 30 and 18 (that is, by 12) and the answer is 46, the number of steps in the stairway, which descends at the rate of 1 step in $1\frac{1}{2}$ seconds. The speed at which I walk on the stairs does not affect the question, as the step from which I alight will reach the bottom at a given moment, whatever I do in the meantime.

30. Sharing a Bicycle

Let Anderson ride $11\frac{1}{9}$ miles, drop the bicycle, and walk the rest of the way. Brown will walk until he picks up the bicycle, and then rides to their destination, getting there at exactly the same time as Anderson. The journey takes them 3 hours 20 minutes. Or you can divide the 20 miles into nine stages of $2\frac{2}{9}$ miles each, and drop the machine at every stage, only you must make Anderson ride at the start. Anderson will then ride each of his five stages in $\frac{2}{9}$ hour and walk each of his four stages in $\frac{5}{9}$ hour, making his total time $3\frac{1}{3}$ hours. Brown will ride each of his four stages in $\frac{5}{18}$ hour and walk each of his five stages in $\frac{4}{9}$ hour, making his total time also $3\frac{1}{3}$ hours. The distances that Anderson and Brown ride respectively must be in the proportion of 5 to 4; the distances they walk in the proportion of 4 to 5.

31. More Bicycling

A. rides $7\frac{11}{27}$ miles, B. rides $1\frac{13}{27}$ miles, and C. rides $11\frac{3}{27}$ miles, making the twenty miles in all. They may ride in any order, only each man should complete his ride in one mount and the second rider must always walk both before and after riding. They will each take $3\frac{8}{9}$ hours on the journey, and therefore will all arrive together.

32. A Side-car Problem

Atkins takes Clarke 40 miles in his car and leaves him to walk the remaining 12 miles. He then rides back and picks up Baldwin at a point 16 miles from the start and takes him to their destination. All three arrive in exactly 5 hours. Or Atkins might take Baldwin 36 miles and return for Clarke, who will have walked his 12 miles. The side-car goes 100 miles in all, with no passenger for 24 miles.

33.   The Despatch-rider

The answer is the square root of twice the square of 40, added to 40. This is 96.568 miles, or, roughly, $96\frac{1}{2}$ miles.

34.   The Two Trains

In 5 seconds both trains (together) go 600 feet, or $81\frac{9}{11}$ miles per hour. In 15 seconds the faster train gains 600 feet, or $27\frac{3}{11}$ miles per hour. From this we get $54\frac{6}{11}$ miles per hour as the rate of the faster train; and it is clear that $27\frac{3}{11}$ miles per hour is the rate of the other.

35.   Pickleminster to Quickville

There are two possible distances that will fit the conditions – 210 miles and 144 miles, only I barred out the latter by the words, 'at an ordinary rate.' With 144 miles A would run 140 miles, while B and D ran 4 miles; so if the latter went 2 miles per hour, the former would have to go 70 miles per hour – rates which are certainly not 'ordinary'! With 210 miles B and D go half the speed of A, and C goes three-quarters the speed of A, so you can give them reasonable rates.

36.   The Damaged Engine

The distance from Anglechester to Clinkerton must be 200 miles. The train went 50 miles at 50 m.p.h. and 150 miles at 30 m.p.h. If the accident had occured 50 miles farther on, it would have gone 100 miles at 50 m.p.h. and 100 miles at 30 m.p.h.

37.   The Puzzle of the Runners

While Brown has only run $\frac{1}{6}$ or $\frac{4}{24}$ of the course, Tompkins has run the remainder $\frac{5}{6}$, less $\frac{1}{8}$, or $\frac{17}{24}$. Therefore Tompkins's pace is $\frac{17}{4}$ times that of Brown. Brown has now $\frac{5}{6}$ of the course to run, whereas Tompkins has only $\frac{1}{6}$. Therefore Brown must go five times as fast as Tompkins, or increase his own speed to five times $\frac{17}{4}$, that is $\frac{85}{4}$ times as fast as he went at first. But the question was not how many times as fast, but 'how much faster', and $\frac{85}{4}$ times as fast is equal to $\frac{81}{4}$ times faster than Brown's original speed. The correct answer is therefore $20\frac{1}{4}$ times faster, though in practice probably impossible.

38. The Two Ships

The error lies in assuming that the average speeds are equal.
They are not. The first ship does a mile in $\frac{1}{12}$ of an hour outwards
and in $\frac{1}{8}$ of an hour homewards. Half of the sum of these fractions is $\frac{5}{48}$.
Therefore the ship's average speed for the four hundred miles is a mile
in $\frac{5}{48}$ of an hour. The average speed of the second ship is a mile in
$\frac{1}{10}$ of an hour.

39. Find the Distance

The distance between the two places must have been 18 miles. The
meeting-points were 10 miles from A—— and 12 miles from B——.
Simply multiply 10 (the first distance) by 3 and deduct the second
distance, 12. Try other distances for the meeting-points (taking care
that the first meeting distance is more than two-thirds of the second)
and you will find the little rule will always work.

40. The Man and the Dog

The dog's speed was 16 miles per hour. The following facts will give
the reader clues to the general solution. The distance remaining to be
walked side by side with the dog was 81 feet, the fourth power of 3
(for the dog returned four times), and the distance to the end of the
road was 625 feet, the fourth power of 5. Then the difference between
the speeds (in miles per hour) of man and dog (that is, 12) and the
sum of the speeds (20) must be in the same ratio, 3 to 5, as is the case.

41. Baxter's Dog

It is obvious that Baxter will overtake Anderson in one hour, for each
will be four miles from the hotel in the same direction. Then, as the
dog has been running uniformly at ten miles an hour during that hour,
he must have run ten miles!

42. Railway Shunting

Make a rough sketch like our diagram and use five counters marked
X, L, R, A and B. The engines are L and R, and the two cars on the
right A and B. The three cars on the left are never separated, so we

call them X. The side-track is marked S. Now, play as follows: R to left, R to S, X L to right, R to left, X L A to left, L takes A to S, L to left, X L to right, R to A, R A to left,

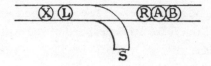

X L B to left, L takes B to S, L to left, L X right away, R A to B, R A B right away. Fourteen moves, because the first and third moves (R to left and X L to right) do not involve a change of direction. It cannot be done in fewer moves.

43. Egg Laying

The answer is half a hen and a half hen; that is, one hen. If one and a half hens lay one and a half eggs in one and a half days, one hen will lay one egg in one and a half days. And a hen who lays better by half will lay one and a half eggs in one and a half days, or one egg per day. So she will lay ten and a half (half a score and a half) in ten and a half days (a week and a half).

44. The Flocks of Sheep

Adam must have possessed 60 sheep, Ben 50, Claude 40 and Dan 30. If the distributions described had taken place, each brother would have then had 45 sheep.

45. Pussy and the Mouse

You have simply to divide the given number by 8. If there be no remainder, then it is the second barrel. If the remainder be 1, 2, 3, 4 or 5, then that remainder indicates the number of the barrel. If you get a remainder greater than 5, just deduct it from 10 and you have the required barrel. Now 500 divided by 8 leaves the remainder 4, so that the barrel marked 4 was the one that contained the mouse.

46. Army Figures

The five brigades contained respectively 5670, 6615, 3240, 2730 and 2772 men. Represent all the fractions with the common denominator 12,012, and the numerators will be 4004, 3432, 7007, 8316, and 8190. Combining all the *different* factors contained in these numbers, we get 7,567,560, which, divided by each number in turn, gives us 1890, 2205, 1080, 910 and 924. To fulfil the condition that the division contained a 'little over 20,000 men', we multiply these by 3 and have the correct total – 21,027.

47. A Critical Vote

There must have been 207 voters in all. At first 115 voted for the motion and 92 against, the majority of 23 being just a quarter of 92. But when the 12 who could not sit down were transferred to the other side, 103 voted for the motion and 104 against. So it was defeated by 1 vote.

48. The House Number

The numbers of the houses on each side will add up alike if the number of the house be 1 and there are no other houses; if the number be 6, with 8 houses in all; if 35, with 49 houses; if 204, with 288 houses; if 1189, with 1681 houses; and so on. But it was known that there were more than 50 and fewer than 500 houses, so we are limited to a single case, and the number of the house must have been 204.

Find the integral solutions of $\dfrac{x^2 + x}{2} = y^2$. Then we get the answers:

x=Number of houses	y=Number of particular house
1	1
8	6
49	35
288	204
1681	1189

and so on.

49.   Another Street Puzzle

On the odd side of the street the house must have been No. 239, and there were 169 houses on that side. On the even side of the street the house must have been No. 408, and there were 288 houses.

In the first case, find integral solution of $2x^2-1=y^2$. Then we get the answers:

x=Number of houses					y=Number of particular house
1	.	.	.	.	1
5	.	.	.	.	7
29	.	.	.	.	41
169	.	.	.	.	239
985	.	.	.	.	1393

and so on.

In the second case, find integral solution of $2(x^2+x)=y^2$. Then we get the answers:

x=Number of houses					y=Number of particular house
1	.	.	.	.	2
8	.	.	.	.	12
49	.	.	.	.	70
288	.	.	.	.	408
1681	.	.	.	.	2378

and so on.

50.   Correcting an Error

Hilda's blunder amounted to multiplying by 49, instead of by 409. Divide the error by the difference (328,320 by 360) and you will get the required number – 912.

51.   Adding their Cubes

The required number is 153. The cubes of 1, 5 and 3 are respectively 1, 125 and 27, and these added together make 153.

52. **Squares and Cubes**

The solution in the smallest possible numbers appears to be this:—

$10^2 - 6^2 = 100 - 36 = 64 = 4^3$.

$10^3 - 6^3 = 1000 - 216 = 784 = 28^2$.

53. **A Common Divisor**

Since the numbers have a common factor plus the same remainder, if the numbers are subtracted from one another in the manner shown below the results must contain the common factor without the remainder

508,811	723,217
480,608	508,811
28,203	214,406

Here the prime factors of 28,203 are 3, 7, 17, 79, and those of 214,406 are 2, 23, 59, 79. And the only factor common to both is 79. Therefore the required divisor is 79, and the common remainder will be found to be 51.

54. **The Rejected Gun**

The experts were right. The gun ought to have fired sixty shots in fifty-nine minutes if it really fired a shot a minute. The time counts from the first shot, so that the second would be fired at the close of the first minute, the third at the close of the second minute, and so on. In the same way, if you put up sixty posts in a straight line, a yard apart, they will extend a length of fifty-nine yards, not sixty.

55. **Odds and Evens**

If the result given is odd, the odd number is in the right hand; if even, the even number is in the right hand. An even number multiplied by either an odd or even number will produce an even number. An odd number multiplied by an odd number will alone produce odd. And if the result given is even, both products added must be even; if the result is odd, one product is even and the other odd. The former result can only happen when the even number is multiplied by the 7; the latter when the odd number is multiplied by 7.

56. The Nine Barrels

There are forty-two different arrangements. The positions of the 1 and 9 are fixed. Always place the 2 beneath the 1. Then, if the 3 be beneath the 2 there are five arrangements. If the 3 be to the right of the 1 there are five arrangements with 4 under the 2, five with 5 under the 2, four with 6 under 2, two with 7 under 2. We have thus twenty-one arrangements in all. But the 2 might have been always to the right of 1, instead of beneath, and then we get twenty-one reversed and reflected arrangements (practically similar), making forty-two in all. Either the 4, 5 or 6 must always be in the centre.

57. A Picture Presentation

Multiply together as many 2's as there are pictures and deduct 1. Thus 2 raised to the tenth power is 1024, and deducting 1 we get 1023 as the correct answer. Suppose there had been only three pictures. Then one can be selected in 3 ways, two in 3 ways, and three in 1 way, making together 7 ways, which is the same as the cube of 2 less 1.

58. A General Election

The answer is 39,147,416 different ways. Add 3 to the number of members (making 618) and deduct 1 from the number of parties (making 3). Then the answer will be the number of ways in which 3 things may be selected from 618. That is

$$\frac{618 \times 617 \times 616}{1 \times 2 \times 3} = 39,147,416 \text{ ways.}$$

The general solution is as follows. Let p=parties and m=members. Then C^{p-r}_{m+p-r}= number of ways.

59. The Magisterial Bench

Apart from any conditions, ten men can be arranged in line in 10 ways=3,628,800. Now how many of these cases are barred? Regard two of a nationality in brackets as one item. (1) Then (E E) (S S) (W W) F I S A can be permuted in 7×2^3 ways=40,320. Remember the two E's can change places within their bracket wherever placed, and so with the S's and the W's. Hence the 2^3. (2) But we may get (E E) (S S) W W F I S A, where the W's are not bracketed, but free. This gives 8×2^2 cases, but we must deduct result (1) or these will be included a second time. Result, 120,960. (3) Deal similarly with the two S's unbracketed. Result, 120,960. (4) Deal again, with the E's unbracketed. Result, 120,960. (5) But we may have (E E) S S W W F I S A, where both S and W are unbracketed. This gives 9×2 cases, but we must deduct results (1), (2) and (3) for reasons that will now be obvious. Result, 443,520. (6) When only S is bracketed, deducting (1), (2) and (4). Result, 443,520. (7) When only W is bracketed, deducting (1), (3) and (4). Result, 443,520. Add these seven results together and you get 1,733,760, which deducted from the number first given above leaves 1,895,040 as the number of ways in which the ten men may sit.

60. The Card Pentagon

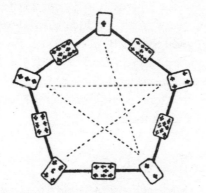

Deal the cards, 1, 2, 3, 4, 5, in the manner indicated by the dotted lines (that is, drop one at every alternate angle in a clockwise direction round the pentagon), and then deal the 6, 7, 8, 9, 10 in the opposite direction, as shown, taking care to start with the 6 on the correct side of the 5. The pips on every side add to 14. If you deal the 6, 7, 8, 9, 10 in the first manner, and the 1, 2, 3, 4, 5 in the second manner, you will get another solution, adding up to 19. Now work with the two sets of numbers, 1, 3, 5, 7, 9, and 2, 4, 6, 8, 10, in the same way and you will get two more solutions, adding respectively to 16 and 17.

There are six different solutions in all. The last two are peculiar. Write in, in the same order, 1, 4, 7, 10, 13 and 6, 9, 12, 15, 18; also write in 8, 11, 14, 17, 20 and 3, 6, 9, 12, 15. Then deduct 10 from every number greater than 10.

61.   A Heptagon Puzzle

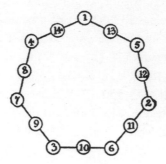

The diagram shows the solution. Starting at the highest point, write in the numbers 1 to 7 in a clockwise direction at alternate points. Then, starting just above the 7, write 8 to 14 successively in the opposite direction, taking every vacant circle in turn. If instead you write in 1, 3, 5, 7, 9, 11, 13, and then 2, 4, 6, 8, 10, 12, 14, you will get a solution with the sides adding to 22 instead of 19. If you substitute for every number in these solutions its difference from 15 you will get the complementary solutions, adding respectively to 26 and 23 (the difference of 19 and 22 from 45).

62.   An Irregular Magic Square

If for the 2 and 15 you substitute 7 and 10, repeated, the square can be formed as shown. Any sixteen numbers can be arranged to form a magic square if they can be written in this way, so that all the horizontal differences are alike and all the vertical differences also alike. The differences here are 3 and 2:

1	10	9	14
13	10	5	6
8	3	16	7
12	11	4	7

1	4	7	10
3	6	9	12
5	8	11	14
7	10	13	16

63. A Magic Square Delusion

Here is an example of such a square.

9	11	18	5	22
3	25	7	14	16
12	19	1	23	10
21	8	15	17	4
20	2	24	6	13

64. Difference Squares

The three examples I give are, I believe, the only cases possible. The difference throughout is 5.

2	1	4
3	5	7
6	9	8

8	1	4
3	5	7
6	9	2

2	1	6
3	5	7
4	9	8

65. Is it Very Easy?

All that is necessary is to push up the second figure in every cell and so form powers of 2, as in the first square. Then the numbers become those in the second square, where all the eight rows give the same product – 4096. Of course, every arithmetician knows that 2^0 equals 1.

2^7	2^0	2^5
2^2	2^4	2^6
2^3	2^8	2^1

128	1	32
4	16	64
8	256	2

66. The Five-pointed Star

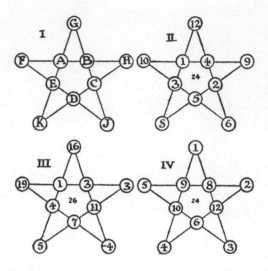

Referring to Diagram I, we will call A, B, C, D, E the 'pentagon', and F, G, H, J, K the 'points.' Write in the numbers 1, 2, 3, 4, 5 in the pentagon in the order shown in Diagram II, where you go round in a clockwise direction, starting with 1 and jumping over a disc to the place for 2, jumping over another for 3, and so on. Now to complete the star for the constant summation of 24, as required, use this simple rule. To find H subtract the sum of B and C from half the constant plus E. That is, subtract 6 from 15. We thus get 9 as the required number for H. Now you are able to write in successively 10 at F (to make 24), 6 at J, 12 at G, and 8 at K. There is your solution.

You can write any five numbers you like in the pentagon, in any order, and with any constant summation that you wish, and you will always get, by the rule shown, the only possible solution for that pentagon and constant. But that solution may require the use of repeated numbers and even negative numbers. Suppose, for example, I make the pentagon 1, 3, 11, 7, 4, and the constant 26, as in Diagram III, then I shall find the 3 is repeated, and the repeated 4 is negative and must be deducted instead of added. You will also find that if we had written our pentagon numbers in Diagram II in any other order we should always get repeated numbers.

Let us confine our attention to solutions with ten different positive whole numbers. Then 24 is the smallest possible constant. A solution for any higher constant can be derived from it. Thus, if we want 26, add 1 at each of the points; if we want 28 add 2 at every point or 1 at every place in both points and pentagon. Odd constants are impossible unless we use fractions. Every solution can be 'turned inside out'. Thus, Diagram IV is simply a different arrangement of Diagram II. Also the four numbers in G, K, D, J may always be changed, if repetitions do not occur. For example, in Diagram II substitute 13, 7, 6, 5 for 12, 8, 5, 6 respectively. Finally, in any solution the constant will be two-fifths of the sum of all the ten numbers. So, if we are given a particular set of numbers we at once know the constant, and for any constant we can determine the sum of the numbers to be used.

67. The Six-pointed Star

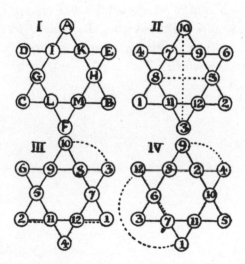

I have insufficient space to explain fully the solution to this interesting problem, but I will give the reader the main points.

1. In every solution the sum of the numbers in the triangle A B C (Fig. 1) must equal the sum of the triangle D E F. This sum may be anything from 12 to 27 inclusive, except 14 and 25, which are impossible. We need only obtain solutions for 12, 13, 15, 16, 17,

18 and 19, because from these all the complementaries, 27, 26, 24, 23, 22, 21 and 20, may be derived by substituting for every number in the star its difference from 13.

2. Every arrangement is composed of three independent diamonds, A G H F, D K B L and E M C I, each of which must always sum to 26.

3. The sum of the numbers in opposite external triangles will always be equal. Thus A I K equals L M F.

4. If the difference between 26 and the triangle sum A B C be added to any number at a point, say A, it will give the sum of the two numbers in the relative positions of L and M. Thus (in Fig. II) 10+13=11+12, and 6+13=8+11.

5. There are six pairs summing to 13; they are 12+1, 11+2, 10+3, 9+4, 8+5, 7+6, and one pair, or two pairs, may occur among the numbers at the points, but never three. The relative positions of these pairs determine the type of solution. In the regular type, as in Fig. 11, A and F and also G and H, as indicated by the dotted lines, always sum to 13, though I subdivide this class. Fig. III and IV are examples of the two irregular types. There are 37 solutions in all (or 74, if we count the complementaries described in my first paragraph), of which 32 are regular and 5 irregular.

Of the 37 solutions, 6 have their points summing to 26. They are as follows:

10	6	2	3	1	4	7	9	5	12	11	8
9	7	1	4	3	2	6	11	5	10	12	8
5	4	6	8	2	1	9	12	3	11	7	10
5	2	7	8	1	3	11	10	4	12	6	9
10	3	1	4	2	6	9	8	7	12	11	5
8	5	3	1	2	7	10	4	11	9	12	6

The first is our Fig. II, and the last but one our Fig. III, so a reference to those diagrams will show how to write the numbers in the star. The reader should write them all out in star form and remember that the 6 are increased to 12 if you also write out their complementaries. The first four are of the regular type and the last two of the irregular. If the reader should be tempted to find all the 37 (or 74) solutions to the puzzle it will help him to know that, where the six points sum to 24, 26, 30, 32, 34, 36, 38, the respective number of solutions is 3, 6, 2, 4, 7, 6, 9, making 37 in all.

68.　The Seven-pointed Star

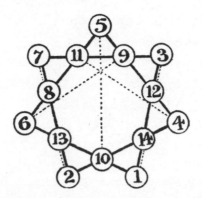

Place 5 at the top point, as indicated in the diagram. Then let the four
numbers in the horizontal line (7, 11, 9, 3) be such that the two
outside numbers shall sum to 10 and the inner numbers to 20, and
that the difference between the two outer numbers shall be twice the
difference between the two inner numbers. Then their
complementaries to 15 are placed in the relative positions shown by
the dotted lines. The remaining four numbers (13, 2, 14, 1) are easily
adjusted. From this fundamental arrangement we can get three others.
(1) Change the 13 with the 1 and the 14 with the 2. (2 and 3)
Substitute for every number in the two arrangements already found its
difference from 15. Thus, 10 for 5, 8 for 7, 4 for 11, and so on. Now,
the reader should be able to construct a second group of four
solutions for himself, by following the rules.

The general solution is too lengthy to be given here in full, but there
are, in all, 56 different arrangements, counting complementaries. I
divide them into three classes. Class I includes all cases like the above
example, where the pairs in the positions of 7-8, 13-2, 3-12, 14-1 all
sum to 15, and there are 20 such cases. Class II includes cases where
the pairs in the *positions* of 7-2, 8-13, 3-1, 12-14 all sum to 15. There
are, again, 20 such cases. Class III includes cases where the pairs in
the *positions* of 7-8, 13-2, 3-1, 12-14 all sum to 15. There are 16 such
cases. Thus we get 56 in all.

69.   Two Eight-pointed Stars

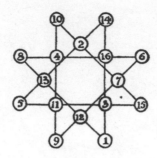

The illustration is the required solution. Every line of four numbers adds up to 34. If you now find any solution to one of the stars, you can immediately transfer it to the other by noting the relative positions in the case given.

I have not succeeded in enumerating the stars of this order. The task is, I think, a particularly difficult one. Perhaps readers may like to attempt the solution.

70.   The Damaged Measure

Let the eight graduation marks divide the 33-inch measure into the following nine sections: 1, 3, 1, 9, 2, 7, 2, 6, 2, and any length can be measured from 1 inch up to 33 inches. Of course, the marks themselves will be at 1, 4, 5, 14, 16, 23, 25 and 31 inches from one end. Another solution is 1, 1, 1, 1, 6, 6, 6, 6, 5.

This puzzle may be solved in, at fewest, sixteen different ways. I have sought a rule for determining the fewest possible marks for any number of inches, and for at once writing out a solution, but a general law governing all the multiplicity of answers has still to be found.

71.   The Six Cottages

If the distances between the cottages are as follows, in the order given, any distance from one mile up to twenty-six inclusive may be found as from one cottage to another: 1, 1, 4, 4, 3, 14 miles round the circular road.

72. A New Domino Puzzle

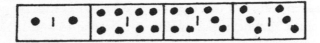

These four dominoes fulfil the conditions. It will be found that, taking contiguous pips, we can make them sum to any number from 1 to 23 inclusive.

73. At the Brook

A					B			
15	16				15	16		
0	16*	15	5*		*15	0	0	11
15	1*	0	5		0	15	15	11
0	1	5	0		15	15	*10	16
1	0	5	16		*14	16	10	0
1	16	15	6*		14	0	0	10
15	2*	0	6		0	14	15	10
0	2	6	0		15	14	*9	16
2	0	6	16		*13	16	9	0
2	16	15	7*		13	0	0	9
15	3*	0	7		0	13	15	9
0	3	7	0		15	13	*8	16
3	0	7	16		*12	16		
3	16	15	8*		12	0		
15	4*	0	8		0	12		
0	4	8	0		15	12		
4	0	8	16		*11	16		
4	16				11	0		

Every line shows a transaction. Thus, in column A, we first fill the 16 measure; then fill the 15 from the 16, leaving 1, if we want it; then empty the 15; then transfer the 1 from 16 to 15; and so on. The asterisks show how to measure successively 1, 2, 3, 4, etc. Or we can start, as in B column, by first filling the 15 and so measure in turn, 14, 13, 12, 11, etc. If we continue A we get B read upwards, or vice versa. It will thus be seen that to measure from 1 up to 7 inclusive in the fewest transactions we must use the method A, but to get from 8 to 14 we must use method B. To measure 8 in the A direction will take 30 transactions, but in the B manner only 28, which is the correct answer. It is a surprising fact that with any two measures that are prime to each other (that have no common divisor, like 15 and 16) we can measure any whole number from 1 up to the largest measure. With measures 4 and 6 (each divisible by 2) we can only measure 2, 4 and 6. With 3 and 9 we could only measure 3, 6 and 9. In our tables the quantities measured come in regular numerical order, because the difference between 15 and 16 is 1. If I had given the measures 9 and 16, under A we should get the order 7, 14, 5, 12, 3, etc., a cyclical difference of 7 (since 16−9=7). After adding 7 to 14 we must deduct 16 to get 5, and after adding 7 to 12 we must deduct 16 to get 3, and so on.

74. A Prohibition Poser

First fill and waste the 7-quart measure 14 times and you will have thrown away 98 and leave 22 quarts in the barrel in 28 transactions. (Filling and emptying are 2 transactions.) Then, fill 7-qt.; fill 5-qt. from 7-qt., leaving 2 in 7-qt.; empty 5-qt.; transfer 2 from 7-qt. to 5-qt.; fill 7-qt.; fill up 5-qt. from 7-qt., leaving 4 in 7-qt.; empty 5-qt.; transfer 4 to 5-qt.; fill 7-qt.; fill up 5-qt. from 7-qt., leaving 6 in 7-qt.; empty 5-qt.; fill 5-qt. from 7-qt., leaving 1 in 7-qt.; empty 5-qt., leaving 1 in 7-qt.; draw off remaining 1-qt. from barrel into 5-qt., and the thing is done in 14 more transactions, making, with the 28 above, 42 transactions. Or you can start by wasting 104 and leaving 16 in the barrel. These 16 can be dealt with in 10 transactions, and the 104 require 32 in the wasting (12 times 7 and 4 times 5 is the quickest way).

75. Prohibition again

Fill 7-qt.; fill 5-qt.; empty 108 quarts from barrel; empty 5-qt. into barrel; fill 5-qt. from 7-qt.; empty 5-qt. into barrel; pour 2 quarts from 7-qt. into 5-qt.; fill 7-qt. from barrel; fill up 5-qt. from 7-qt.; empty 5-qt. into barrel; pour 4 quarts from 7-qt. into 5-qt.; fill 7-qt. from barrel; fill up 5-qt. from 7-qt.; throw away contents of 5-qt.; fill 5-qt. from barrel; throw away 5 quarts from 5-qt.; empty 1 quart from barrel into 5-qt. The feat is thus performed in 17 transactions – the fewest possible.

76. The False Scales

If the scales had been false on account of the pans being unequally weighted, then the true weight of the pudding would be 154 oz., and it would have weighed 130 oz. in one pan and 178 oz. in the other. Half the sum of the apparent weights (the arithmetic mean) equals 154. But the illustration showed that the pans weighed evenly, and that the error was in the unequal lengths of the arms of the balance. Therefore, the apparent weights were 121 oz. and 169 oz., and the real weight 143 oz. Multiply the apparent weights together and we get the square of 143 – the geometric mean. The lengths of the arms were in the ratio 11 to 13.

If we call the true weight x in each case, then we get the equations:

$$\frac{\left(\frac{9}{11}x + 4\right) + \left(\frac{9}{11}x + 52\right)}{2} = x, \text{ and } x = 154.$$

$$\sqrt{\left(\frac{9}{11}x + 4\right) \times \left(\frac{9}{11}x + 52\right)} = x, \text{ and } x = 143.$$

77. Weighing the Goods

Since one canister weighs an ounce, the first illustration shows that in one pan eight packets equal three ounces, and, therefore, one packet will weigh three-eighths of an ounce. The second illustration shows that in the other pan one packet equals six ounces. Multiply $\frac{3}{8}$ by 6 and we get $\frac{9}{4}$, the square root of which is $\frac{3}{2}$, or $1\frac{1}{2}$ oz. as the real weight of one packet. Therefore, eight packets weigh twelve ounces, which is the correct answer.

78. Monkey and Pulley

We find the age of the monkey works out at $1\frac{1}{2}$ years, and the age of the mother $2\frac{1}{2}$ years, the monkey therefore weighing $2\frac{1}{2}$ lb., and the weight the same. Then we soon discover that the rope weighed $1\frac{1}{4}$ lb., or 20 oz.; and, as a foot weighed 4 oz., the length of the rope was 5 feet.

79. Weighing the Baby

It is important to notice that the man, baby and dog weigh together 180 lb., as recorded on the dial in the illustration. Now, the difference between 180 and 162 is 18, which equals twice the weight of the dog, whose weight is 9 lb. Therefore the baby weighs 30 lb., since 30 less 70 per cent is 9.

80. Packing Cigarettes

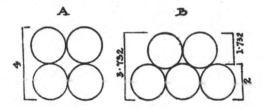

Say the diameter of a cigarette is 2 units and that 8 rows of 20 each, as in Fig. A (that is, 160 cigarettes), exactly fit the box. The inside length of the box is therefore 40 and the depth 16. Now, if we place 20 in the bottom row, and, instead of placing 20 in the next row, we drop 19 into the position shown in Fig. B, we save .268 (i.e. $2 - \sqrt{3}$) in height. This second row, and every additional row of 20 and 19 alternately, will increase the height by 1.732. Therefore, we shall have 9 rows reaching to a height of $2+8\times1.732$ or 15.856, which is less than our depth of 16. We shall thus increase the number of cigarettes by 20 (through the additional row), and reduce it by 4 (1 in each row of 19), making a net increase of 16 cigarettes.

81. Fallacious Reasoning

The fallacy is in moving from

$$(x + a)(x - a) = a(x - a)$$

to

$$x + a = a$$

as, given that $x = a$, dividing by $(x - a)$ means dividing by zero.

82. The Sheep

7 and 5.

83. Careful Division

The parts are 8, 12, 20 and 5.

Solutions: Chapter 3.
Geometrical Puzzles

1.   The Square Table-top

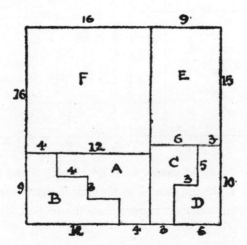

The illustration shows the simplest, and I think the prettiest, solution in six pieces. Move piece A up a step on B and you have the original piece 12×12. Move C up a step on D and the two pieces will join E and form the square 15×15. The piece 16×16 is not cut.

2.   A New Cutting-out Puzzle

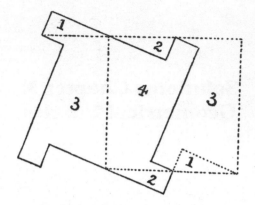

Make the cuts as shown in the illustration and fit the pieces into the places enclosed by the dotted lines.

3.   The Squares of Veneer

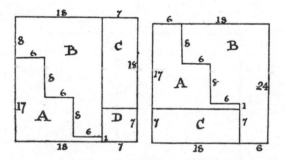

The sides of the two squares must be 24 inches and 7 inches respectively. Make the cuts as in the first diagram and the pieces A, B and C will form a perfect square as in the second diagram. The square D is cut out intact.

4.   Dissecting the Moon

The illustration shows that the five cuts can be so cunningly made as to produce as many as twenty-one pieces.

Calling the number of cuts n, then in the case of a circle the maximum number of pieces will be $\dfrac{n^2 + n}{2} + 1$, but in the case of the crescent it will be $\dfrac{n^2 + 3n}{2} + 1$.

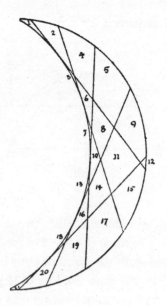

5.   Dissecting the Letter E

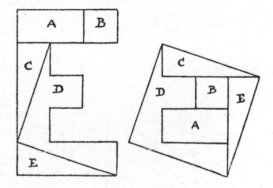

The illustration shows how to cut the letter into five pieces that will fit together to form a perfect square. It can be done in four pieces if you are allowed to turn pieces over. Readers may like to find for themselves the method.

6.   Hexagon to Square

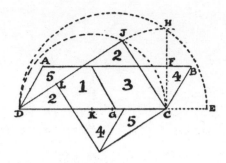

Cut your hexagon in half and place the two parts together to form the figure A B C D. Continue the line D C to E, making C E equal to the height C F. Then, with the point of your compasses at G, describe the semicircle D H E, and draw the line C H perpendicular to D E. Now, C H is the mean proportional between D C and C E, and therefore the side of the required square. From C describe the arc H J, and with the point of your compasses at K describe the semicircle D J C. Draw C J and D J. Make J L equal to J C, and complete the square. The rest requires no explanation.

7.   Squaring a Star

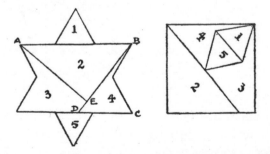

I give the very neat solution by Mr E. B. Escott, of Chicago, Illinois. The five pieces of the star form a perfect square. Find side of equal square (a mean proportional between A B and B C) and make B D equal to such side. Drop perpendicular from A on B D at E and A E will equal B D. The rest is obvious.

8.   The Mutilated Cross

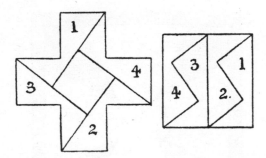

The illustration shows clearly how to cut the mutilated cross into four pieces to form a square. Just continue each side of the square until you strike a corner, and there you are!

9.   The Victoria Cross

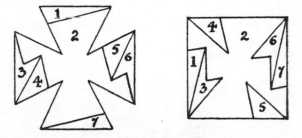

The illustration will show how to cut the cross into seven pieces to form a square.

10.   The Maltese Cross

Cut the star in four pieces across the centre, and place them in the four corners of the frame. Then you have a perfect Maltese Cross in white, as indicated.

11.   The Pirates' Flag

The illustration will show that the flag need only be cut in two pieces – along the zigzag line. If the lower piece is then moved up one step we shall get a flag with the required ten stripes.

12.   The Crescent and the Star

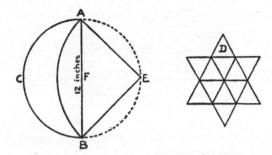

Though we cannot square a circle, certain portions of a circle may be squared, as Hippocrates of old first discovered. If we draw the circle in the diagram and then, with the point of the compasses at E, draw the arc B A, the area of the lune or crescent is exactly the same as the area of the triangle A B E. As we know the line A B to be 12 inches, the area of the triangle (and therefore of the crescent) is obviously 36 square inches. Also, as the triangle D is known to contain 3 square inches, the star, which is built up of twelve such triangles, contains 36 square inches. Therefore the areas of the crescent and the star were exactly the same.

13.   The Patchwork Quilt

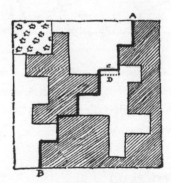

Except for my warning, the reader might have supposed that the dark zigzag line from A to B would solve the puzzle. But it will not, because the pieces are not of the same size and shape. It would be all right if we could go along the dotted line D instead of C, but that would mean cutting a piece. We must cut out all the shaded portion in one piece, which will exactly match the other. One portion of the patchwork is drawn in just to guide the eye when comparing with the original.

14.   The Improvised Draughts-board

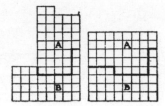

The illustration shows how to cut into two pieces, A and B, that will fit together and form the square board.

15.   Tessellated Pavements

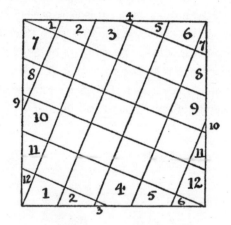

The illustration shows how the square space may be covered with twenty-nine square tiles by laying down seventeen whole and cutting each of the remaining twelve tiles in two parts. Two parts having a similar number form a whole tile.

16.   The Ribbon Pentagon

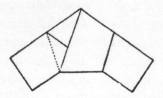

Tie a ribbon of paper into a simple, ordinary knot and press flat, as shown in the illustration, and fold back at the dotted line. Then you have a regular pentagon, obtained with very little trouble.

17. Paper Folding

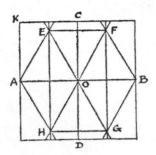

Fold through the mid-points of the opposite sides and get the lines A O B and C O D. Also fold E H and F G, bisecting A O and O B. Turn over A K so that K lies on the line E H, at the point E, and then fold A E and E O G. Similarly find H and fold A H and H O F. Now fold B F, B G, E F and H G, and E F B G H A E is the regular hexagon required.

18. Folding a Pentagon

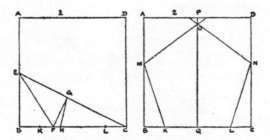

Fold A B on itself and find the mid-point E. Fold through E C. Lay E B on E C and fold so as to get E F and F G. Make C H equal to C G. Find K, the mid-point on B H, and make C L equal to B K. B C is said to be divided in medial section, and we have found K L, the side of the pentagon. Now (see second diagram) lay K M and L N equal to K L, so that M and N may lie on B A and C D respectively. Fold P Q and lay M O and N O equal to K M and L N. Then K M O N L is the pentagon required.

19. Making an Octagon

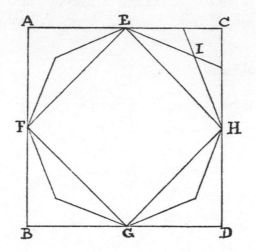

By folding the edge C D over A B we can crease the middle points E and G. In a similar way we can find the points F and H, and then crease the square E H G F. Now fold C H on E H and E C on E H, and the point where the creases cross will be I. Proceed in the same way at the other three corners, and the regular octagon, as shown, will be marked out by the creases, and may be at once cut out.

20. Making a Pentagon

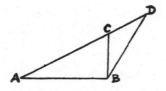

Let A B be the required 1 inch in length. Make B C perpendicular to A B and equal to half A B. Draw A C, which produce until C D equals C B. Then join B D, and B D is the radius of the circumscribing circle. If you draw the circle the sides of the pentagon can be marked off – 1 inch in length.

21. Drawing an Oval

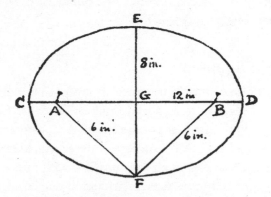

Draw the two lines C D and E F at right angles (C D being equal to the required length, 12 inches, and E F to the required breadth, 8 inches), intersecting midway. Find the points A and B, so that A F and F B each equal half the length C D, that is 6 inches, and place your pins at A and B, making the length of your loop of string equal to A B F A. Say the distance C A $=x$. Then, when the pencil is at F the length of string is $12+(12-2x)=24-2x$, and when the pencil is at C the length of string is $2(12-x)=24-2x$ also, proving the correctness of the solution.

22. With Compasses Only

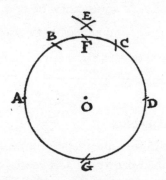

In order to mark off the four corners of a square, using the compasses only, first describe a circle, as in the diagram. Then, with the compasses open at the same distance, and starting from any point, A, in the circumference, mark off the points B, C, D. Now, with the centres A and D and the distance A C, describe arcs at E, and the distance E O is the side of the square sought. If, therefore, we mark off F and G from A with this distance, the points A, F, D, G will be the four corners of a perfect square.

23.   Lines and Squares

If you draw fifteen lines in the manner shown in the diagram, you will have formed exactly one hundred squares. There are forty with sides of the length A B, twenty-eight of the length A C, eighteen of the length A D, ten of the length A E, and four squares with sides of the length A F, making one hundred in all. It is possible with fifteen straight lines to form 112 squares, but we were restricted to one hundred. With fourteen straight lines you cannot form more than ninety-one squares.

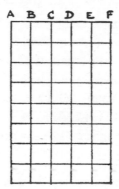

The general formula is that with n straight lines we can form as many as $\dfrac{(n-3)\,(n-1)\,(n+1)}{24}$ squares if n be odd, and $\dfrac{(n-2)\,n\,(n-1)}{24}$ if n be even.

If there are m straight lines at right angles to n straight lines, m being less than n, then $\dfrac{m(m-1)\,(3n-m-1)}{6}$ = number of squares.

24.   The Circle and Discs

In our diagram the dotted lines represent the circumference of the red circle and an inscribed pentagon. The centre of both is C. Find D, a point equidistant from A, B and C, and with radius A D draw the circle A B C. Five discs of this size will cover the circle if placed with their centres at D, E, F, G and H. If the diameter of the large circle is 6 inches, the diameter of the discs is a little less than 4 inches, or 4 inches 'to the nearest half-inch'. It requires a little care and practice correctly to place the five discs without shifting, unless you make some secret markings that would not be noticed by others. I will just add that covering is possible if the ratio of the two diameters exceeds .6094185, and impossible if the ratio is less than .6094180. In my case below, where all five discs touch the centre, the ratio is .6180340.

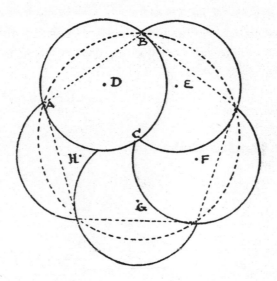

25. Mr Grindle's Garden

The rule is this. When the four sides are in arithmetical progression the greatest area is equal to the square root of their continual product. The square root of 7×8×9×10 is 70.99, or very nearly 71 square rods. This is the correct answer.

26. The Garden Path

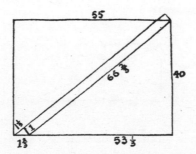

The area of the path is exactly $66\frac{2}{3}$ square yards, which is clearly seen if you imagine the little triangular piece cut off at the bottom and removed to the top right-hand corner. Here is the proof. The area of the garden is 55×40=2200. And $(53\frac{1}{3} \times 40)+66\frac{2}{3}$ also equals 2200. Finally, the sum of the squares of $53\frac{1}{3}$ and 40 must equal the square of $66\frac{2}{3}$, as it does.

The general solution is as follows: Call breadth of rectangle B, length of rectangle L, width of path C, and length of path x.

Then $x = \dfrac{\pm B\sqrt{\left(B^2 - C^2\right)\left(B^2 + L^2\right)} + C^2 L^2 - BCL}{B^2 - C^2}$

In the case given above $x=66\frac{2}{3}$, from which we find the length $53\frac{1}{3}$.

27. The Garden Bed

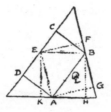

Bisect the three sides in A, B and E. If you join A B and drop the perpendiculars A D and B C, then A B C D will be the largest possible rectangle and exactly half the area of the triangle. The two other solutions, F E A G and K E B H, would also serve (all these rectangles being of the same area) except for the fact that they would enclose the tree. This applies to any triangle with acute angles, but in the case of a right-angled triangle there are only two equal ways of proceeding.

28. A Fence Problem

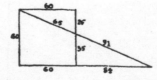

The diagram gives all the measurements. Generally a solution involves a biquadratic equation, but as I said the answer was in '*exact feet*,' the square of 91 is found to be the sum of two squares in only one way –

the squares of 84 and 35. Insert these numbers as shown and the rest is easy and proves itself. The required distance is 35 feet.

29.   A New Match Puzzle

The smallest possible number is 36 matches. We can form triangle and square with 12 and 24 respectively, triangle and pentagon with 6 and 30, triangle and hexagon with 6 and 30, square and pentagon with 16 and 20, square and hexagon with 12 and 24, and pentagon and hexagon with 30 and 6. The pairs of numbers may be varied in all cases except the fourth and last. There cannot be fewer than 36. The triangle and hexagon require a number divisible by 3: the square and hexagon require an even number. Therefore the number must be divisible by 6, such as 12, 18, 24, 30, 36, but this condition cannot be fulfilled for a pentagon and hexagon with fewer than 36 matches.

30.   Hurdles and Sheep

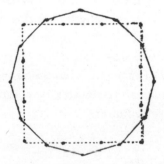

If the enclosure is to be rectangular, the nearer the rectangle approaches to the form of a square the greater will be the area. But the greatest area of all will always be when the hurdles are arranged in the form of a regular polygon, inscribed in a circle, and if this can be done in more than one way the greatest area will be when there are as many sides as hurdles. Thus, the hexagon given on page 56 had a greater area than the triangle. The twelve-sided figure or regular dodecagon therefore encloses the largest possible area for twelve hurdles – room for about eleven sheep and one-fifth. Eleven hurdles would only accommodate a maximum of about nine and nine-twenty-fifths, so that twelve hurdles are necessary for ten sheep. If you arrange the hurdles in the form of a square, as shown by the dotted lines, you only get room for nine sheep.

31. The Four Draughtsmen

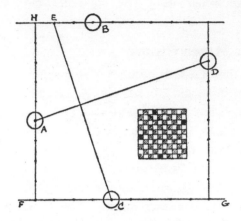

Draw a line from A to D. Then draw C E perpendicular to A D, and
equal in length to A D. Then E will be the centre of another square.
Draw a line from E to B and extend it on both sides. Also draw a line
F G through C and parallel to E B and the lines through A and D
perpendicular to E B and F G. Now, as H is the centre of a corner
square, we can mark off the length H E all round the square and we
find the board is 10 × 10. If the size of the men were not given we
might subdivide into more squares, but the men would be too large for
the squares. As the distance between the centres of squares is the same
as the width of the squares, we can now complete the board with ease,
as shown in the diagram inset.

32. A Crease Problem

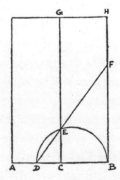

Bisect A B in C and draw the line C G, parallel to B H. Then bisect A
C in D and draw the semicircle D B, cutting the line C G in E. Now

the line D E F gives the direction of the shortest possible crease under the conditions.

33. The Six Submarines

It will be seen from the illustration that this puzzle is absurdly easy – when you know how to do it! And yet I have not the slightest doubt that many readers found it a hard nut to crack. It will be seen that every match undoubtedly touches every other match.

34. Economy in String

The total length of string that passes along the length, breadth, or depth must in every case be the same to allow of the maximum dimensions – that is, 4 feet. When the reader is told this, or has found it for himself (and I think the point will be found interesting), the rest is exceedingly easy. For the string passes 2 times along length, 4 times along breadth and 6 times along depth. Therefore 4 feet divided by 2, 4 and 6 will give us 2 feet, 1 foot and $\frac{2}{3}$ foot respectively for the length, breadth, and depth of the largest possible parcel.

The following general solution is by Mr. Alexander Fraser. Let the string pass a times along length x, b times along breadth y, and c times along depth z, and let length of string be m.

Then $ax+by+cz=m$. Find maximum value of xyz.

First find maximum area of xy.

Put $ax + by = n, x = \dfrac{n - by}{a}, xy = \dfrac{n}{a}y\dfrac{b}{a}y^2, \dfrac{dxy}{dy} = \dfrac{n}{a} - \dfrac{2b}{a}y = 0,$

$$\therefore y = \dfrac{n}{2b}, \text{ or } by = \dfrac{n}{2}$$

$\therefore ax$ also $= \dfrac{n}{2}$, and $ax = by$.

Similarly, $ax = by = cz = \dfrac{m.}{3}$

$\therefore x = \dfrac{m}{3^a}$, $y = \dfrac{m}{3^b}$, $z = \dfrac{m}{3^c}$, and $xyz = \dfrac{m^3.}{27abc.}$

In the case of the puzzle, $a=2$, $b=4$, $c=6$, $m=12$.

$\therefore x = 2$, $y = 1$, $z = \frac{2}{3}$.

$xyz = 1\frac{1}{3}$.

35.   The Stone Pedestal

The cube of a square number is always a square. Thus, the cube of 1 is 1, the square of 1.

The cube of 4 is 64, the square of 8.

The cube of 9 is 729, the square of 27.

The cube of 16 is 4096, the square of 64.

And so on.

We were told to look at the illustration. If there were one block in pedestal and one in base, the base would be entirely covered, which it was not. If 64 in pedestal and base, the side of the former would measure 4 feet, and the side of square 8 feet. A glance will show that this is wrong. But 729 blocks in each case is quite in agreement with the illustration, for the width of the pedestal (9 feet) would be one-third of the width of the square (27 feet). In all the successive higher cases the square will be increasingly too large for the pedestal to be in agreement with the illustration.

36.   The Bricklayer's Task

A glance at the illustration will show that if you could cut off the portion of wall marked 1 and place it in the position indicated by 2, you would have a piece of straight wall, B C, enclosed by the dotted lines, exactly similar to the wall A B. Therefore, both men were wrong, and the price should be the same for the portion of wall that went over the hill as for the part on the level. Of course, the reader will see at a glance that this will only apply within a certain limitation. But an actual drawing of the wall was given.

37.   A Cube Paradox

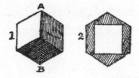

It is a curious fact that a cube can be passed through another cube of smaller dimensions. Suppose a cube to be raised so that its diagonal A B is perpendicular to the plane on which it rests, as in Figure 1. Then the resulting projection will be a regular hexagon, as shown. In Figure 2 the square hole is cut for the passage of a cube of the same dimensions. But it will be seen that there is room for cutting a hole that would pass a cube of even larger dimensions. Therefore, the one through which I cut a hole was not, as the reader may have hastily supposed, the larger one, but the smaller! Consequently, the larger cube would obviously remain the heavier. This could not happen if the smaller were passed through the larger.

38.   The Cardboard Box

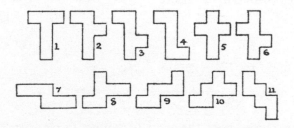

There are eleven different shapes in all, if turning over is allowed, and they are as shown. If the outside of the box is blue and the inside

white, and every possible shape has to be laid out with white
uppermost, then there are twenty different ways, for all except Nos. 1
and 5 can be reversed to be different.

39.   The Austrian Pretzel

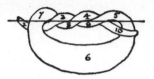

The Pretzel may be divided into as many as ten pieces by one straight
cut of the knife in the direction indicated in the illustration.

40.   Cutting the Cheese

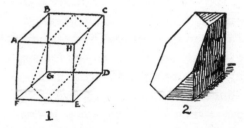

Mark the mid-points in B C, C H, H E, E F, F G and G B. Then
insert the knife at the top and follow the direction indicated by the
dotted plane. Then the two surfaces will each be a perfect hexagon,
and the piece on the right will, in perspective, resemble Figure 2.

41.   A Tree-planting Puzzle

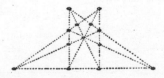

The illustration shows the graceful manner of planting the trees so as
to get nine rows with four trees in every row.

42.   The Way to Tipperary

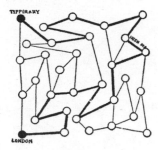

The thick line in the illustration shows a route from London to Tipperary in eighteen moves. It is absolutely necessary to include the stage marked 'Irish Sea' in order to perform the journey in an even number of stages.

43.   Marking a Tennis Court

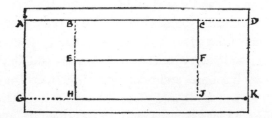

The ten points lettered in the illustration are all 'odd nodes', that is points from which you can go in an odd number of directions – three. Therefore we know that five lines (one-half of 10) will be required to draw the figure. The dotted lines will be the four shortest possible between nodes. Note that you cannot here use a node twice or it would be an improvement to make E H and C F dotted lines instead of C D and G H. Having fixed our four shortest lines, the remainder may all be drawn in one continuous line from A to K, as shown. When you get to D you must run up to C and back to D, from G go to H and back, and so on. Or you can wait until you get to C and go to D and back, etc. The dotted lines will thus be gone over twice and the method shown gives us the minimum distance that must be thus repeated.

44.   The Nine Bridges

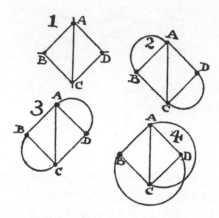

Transform the map as follows. Reduce the four islands, A, B, C and D, to mere points and extend the bridges into lines, as in Fig. 1, and the conditions are unchanged. If you link A and B for outside communication, and also C and D, the conditions are as in Fig. 2; if you link A and D, and also B and C, you get Fig. 3; if you link A and C, and also B and D, you get Fig. 4. In each case B and D are 'odd nodes' (points from which you can proceed in an odd number of ways, three), so in every route you must start and finish at B or D, to go over every line once, and once only. Therefore, Tompkins must live at B or D: we will say B, and place Johnson at D. There are 44 routes by scheme 2, 44 by scheme 3, and 44 by scheme 4, making 132 in all, not counting reverse routes as different. Taking Fig. 2, and calling the outside curved lines O, if you start B O A B, B O A C, B A O B, or B A C, there are 6 ways of continuing in each case. If you start B O A D, B A D, B C O D, B C A or B C D, there are always 4 ways of continuing. In the case of Fig. 3, B O C A, B O C B, B C A, or B C O B give 6 ways. B O C D, B A O D, B A C, B A D, or B C D give 4 ways each. Similarly in the case of Fig. 4.

45. **The Five Regiments**

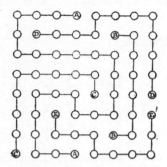

In the illustration, in which the roads not used are omitted for the sake of clearness, the routes of the five regiments are shown. No two regiments ever go along the same road.

46. **Going to Church**

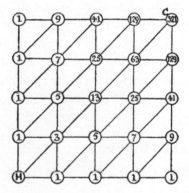

Starting from the house, H, there is only one way of getting to each of the points in a northerly direction, and also going direct east, so I write in the figure 1, as shown. Now take the second column, and you will find that there are three ways of going to the second point from the bottom, five ways to the next above, seven to the next, and so on, continually adding two. The same applies to the second row from the bottom. Write in these numbers. Then the central point of all can be reached in thirteen ways, because we can enter it either from the point below that can be reached in five ways, from the point to the left that can also be reached in five ways, or from the diagonal point below that can be reached in three ways, making together thirteen. So all we have to do is to write in turn at every point the sum of those three numbers from which it can be immediately reached. We thus find that the total number of different routes from H to C is 321.

47.   A Motor-car Puzzle

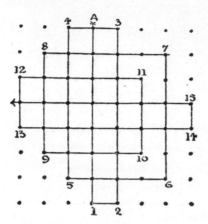

It will be seen from the illustration (where the roads not used are omitted) that the traveller can go as far as 70 miles in fifteen turnings. The turnings are all numbered in the order in which they are taken. He never visits nineteen of the towns. He might visit them all in fifteen turnings, never entering any town twice, and end at A, from which he starts, but such a tour would only take him 64 miles.

48.   The Fly and the Honey

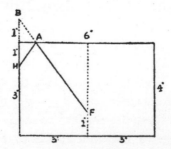

The drop of honey is represented by H, the fly by F. The fly clearly has to go over the edge to the other side. Now, imagine we are dealing with a cylinder of cardboard. If we cut it we can lay it out flat. If we then extend the line of the side 1 inch to B, the line F B will cut the edge at A, which will be the point at which the fly must go over. The shortest distance is thus the hypotenuse of a right-angled triangle, whose height is 4 and base 3. This we know is 5, so that the fly has to go exactly 5 inches.

49. The Russian Motor-cyclists

The two distances given were 15 miles and 6 miles. Now, all you need do is to divide 15 by 6 and add 2, which gives us $4\frac{1}{2}$. Now divide 15 by $4\frac{1}{2}$, and the result ($3\frac{1}{3}$ miles) is the required distance between the two points. This pretty little rule applies to all such cases where the road forms a right-angled triangle. A simple solution by algebra will show why that constant 2 is added. And we can prove the answer in this way. The three sides of the triangle are 15 miles, $9\frac{1}{3}$ miles (6 plus $3\frac{1}{3}$ miles) and $17\frac{2}{3}$ miles (to make it 21 miles each way). Multiply by 3 to get rid of the fractions, and we have 45, 28 and 53. Now, if the square of 45 (2025) added to the square of 28 (784) equal the square of 53 (2809) then it is correct – and it will be found that they do so.

50. Those Russian Cyclists Again

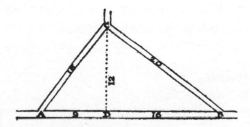

The diagram gives all the correct distances. All the General had to do was to square Pipipoff's 60 miles (3600) and divide by twice the sum of that 60 and Sliponsky's 12 miles – that is, by 144. Doing it in his head, he, of course, saw that this is the same as dividing 300 by 12, which at once gave him the correct answer, 25 miles, as the distance from A to B.

51.   The Despatch-rider in Flanders

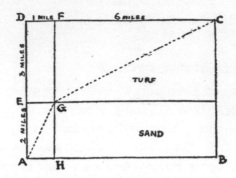

Of course, a straight line from A to C would not be the quickest route. It would be quicker to ride from A to E and then direct to C. The quickest possible route of all is that shown in the diagram by the dotted line from A to G (exactly 1 mile from E) and then direct to C.

It is necessary that the sine of the angle F G C shall be double the sine of A G H. In the first case the sine is 6 divided by the square root of 6^2+3^2, which is 6 divided by the square root of 45, or the same as 2 divided by the square root of 5. In the second case the sine is 1 divided by the square root of 1^2+2^2, which is 1 divided by the square root of 5. Thus the first is exactly double the second.

52.   Land Division

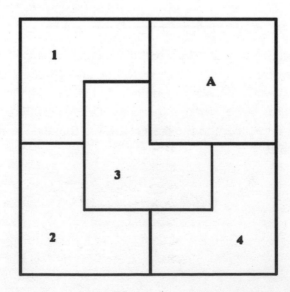

53.   The Orchard

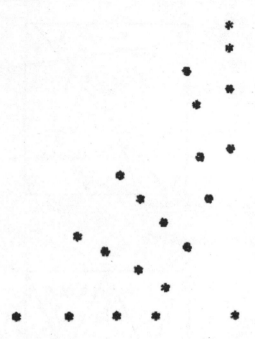

54.   Drawing an Oval

To describe an oval with one sweep of the compasses, all you need do is first to wrap your paper round a wine bottle, canister, or other cylindrical object. Then it will be found easy enough.

55.   The Four Houscholders

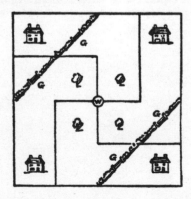

The simplest, though not the only solution, is that shown in our illustration.

56. The Five Fences

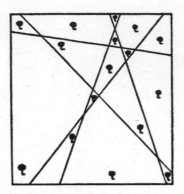

57. The Farmer's Sons

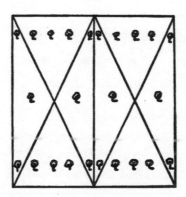

The illustration shows a simple solution to this puzzle. The land is divided into eight equal parts, each containing three trees.

58. Avoiding the Mines

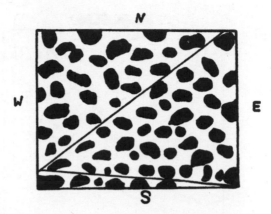

The illustration shows the passage through the mines in two straight courses.

59. Six Straight Fences

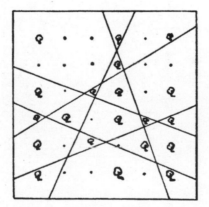

The six straight fences are so drawn that every one of the twenty trees is in a separate enclosure. We stated that twenty-two trees might be so enclosed in the square by six straight fences if their positions were more accommodating. We will here state that in such a case every line must cross every other line without any two crossings coinciding. As there are in our puzzle only twenty trees, this is not necessary, and it will be seen that four of the fences cross only four others instead of five.

60. Footprints in the Snow

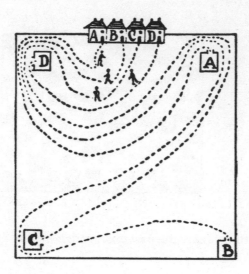

The illustration explains itself.

Solutions: Chapter 4. Logical and Lateral Thinking Puzzles

1. **Crossing the Ferry**

   The puzzle can be solved in as few as nine crossings, as follows: (1) Mr and Mrs Webster cross. (2) Mrs Webster returns. (3) Mother and daughter-in-law cross. (4) Mr Webster returns. (5) Father-in-law and son cross. (6) Daughter-in-law returns. (7) Mr Webster and daughter-in-law cross. (8) Mr Webster returns. (9) Mr and Mrs Webster cross.

2. **Missionaries and Cannibals**

   Call the three missionaries M m m, and the three cannibals C c c, the capitals denoting the missionary and the cannibal who can row the boat. Then C c row across; C returns with the boat; C c row across; C returns; M m row across; M c return; M C row across; M c return; M m row across; C returns; C c row across; C returns; C c row across; and all have crossed the river within the conditions stated.

3.   A Domino Square

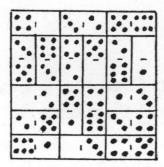

The illustration explains itself. The eighteen dominoes are arranged so as to form the required square, and it will be found that in no column or row is a number repeated. There are, of course, many other ways of doing it.

4.   A Domino Star

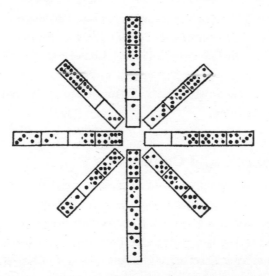

The illustration shows a correct solution. The dominoes are placed together according to the ordinary rule, the pips in every ray sum to 21, and the central numbers are 1, 2, 3, 4, 5, 6 and two blanks.

5.   Domino Groups

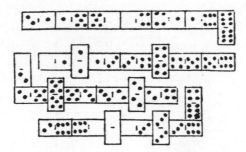

The illustration shows one way in which the dominoes may be laid out so that, when the line is broken in four lengths of seven dominoes each, every length shall contain forty-two pips.

6.   Les Quadrilles

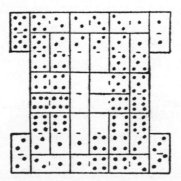

The illustration shows a correct solution, the two blank squares being on the inside. If in the example shown on page 76 all the numbers had not happened to be found somewhere on the edge, it would have been an easy matter, for we should have had merely to exchange that missing number with a blank wherever found. There would thus have been no puzzle. But in the circumstances it is impossible to avail oneself of such a simple manoeuvre.

7.   A Puzzle with Cards

Arrange the pack in the following order face downwards with 9 of Clubs at the top and 5 of Spades at bottom: 9 C., Jack D., 5 C., ace D., King H., King S., 7 H., 2 D., 6 S., Queen D., 10 S., ace S., 3 C., 3 D., 8 C., King D., 8 H., 7 C., 4 D., 2 S., ace H., ace C., 7 S., 5 D., 9 H., 2 H., Jack S., 6 D., Queen C., 6 C., 10 H., 3 S., 3 H., 7 D., 4 C., 2 C., 8 S., Jack H., 4 H., 8 D., Jack C., 4 S., Queen S., King C., 9 D., 5 H., 10 C., Queen H., 10 D., 9 S., 6 H., 5 S.

8.   A Card Trick

Every pile must contain thirteen cards, less the value of the bottom card. Therefore, thirteen times the number of piles less the sum of the bottom cards, and plus the number of cards left over, must equal fifty-two, the number in the pack. Thus thirteen times the number of piles plus number of cards left over, less fifty-two, must equal the sum of the bottom cards. Or, which is the same thing, the number of piles less four, multiplied by thirteen, and plus the cards left over gives the answer as stated. The algebraically inclined reader can easily express this in terms of his familiar symbols.

9.   A Golf Competition Puzzle

The players may be paired and arranged as follows:

	ROUNDS				
	1	2	3	4	5
1ST LINKS	BC	BF	EF	CE	AD
2ND LINKS	FA	CD	CA	DF	BE
3RD LINKS	DE	EA	DB	AB	CF

10.   Cricket Scores

The four innings must have secured 128, 96, 72 and 54 runs respectively. Therefore, the Muddletonians scored 200 against their opponents' 150 and beat them by 50 runs.

11. Football Results

We see at once from the table that England beat Ireland and drew with Wales. As E. scored 2 goals to 0 in these games, they must have won 2 – 0 and drawn 0 – 0. This disposes of E. and leaves three games, W. *v.* I., S. *v.* I., and S. *v.* W., to be determined. Now, S. had only 1 goal scored against them – by W. or I. I. scored only 1 goal, and that must have been against W. or S. Assume it was against S. In that case W. did not score against S. But W. scored 3 goals altogether; therefore these must have been scored against I. We find I. had 6 goals against them: 2 scored by E., as shown, 3 by W. (if we assume that I. scored *v.* S.), and the remaining goal was scored by S. But, as we have just assumed I. scored 1 goal against S., the match would have been drawn. It was won by S., and therefore I. could not have scored against S. Thus the goal against S. must have been scored by W. And as W. scored 3 goals, the other two must have been *v.* I., who must have scored their only goal against W. Thus S. beat W. by 2 – 1 and I. by 2 – 0, while W. won by 2 – 1 *v.* I.

12. Noughts and Crosses

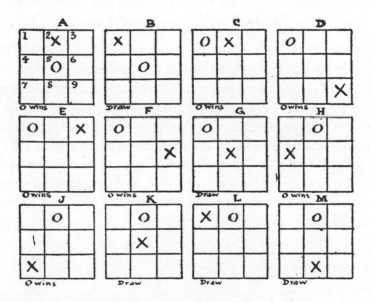

Number the board, as in Fig. A. Mr Nought (the first player) can open in one of three ways: he can play to the centre, 5, or to a corner, 1, 3, 7 or 9, or to a side, 2, 4, 6 or 8. Let us take these openings in turn. If he leads with a centre, then Mr Cross has the option of a corner or a side. If he takes a side, such as 2 in Fig. A, then Nought plays 1 and 4 successively (or 1 and 7), and wins. Cross must take a corner, as in Fig. B, and then Nought cannot do better than draw. If Nought leads with a corner, say 1, Cross has five different replies, as in Figs. C, D, E, F and G (for 4 here is the same as 2, 7 the same as 3, and 8 the same as 6). If he plays as in Fig. C, Nought wins with 5 and 4; if he plays as in D, Nought wins with 7 and 3; if as in E, Nought wins with 9 and 7; if as in F, Nought wins with 5 and 3. Cross is compelled to take the centre, as in Fig. G, to save the game, for this will result in a draw. If Nought opens with a side, say 2, as in Figs. H, J, K, L and M, and Cross plays as in H, Nought wins with 5 and 1; and if he plays as in J, Nought wins with 1 and 5. Cross must play as in K, L or M to secure a draw.

I have thus shown the play for Nought to win in seven cases where Cross makes a bad first move, but I have not space to prove the draws in the remaining five positions B, G, K, L and M. But the reader can easily try each of these cases for himself and be convinced that neither player can win without the bad play of his opponent. Of course, either player can throw away the game. For example, if in Fig. L Nought stupidly plays 3 on his second move, Cross can play 7 and 9 and win. Or if Nought plays 8, Cross can play 5 and 7 and win.

Now, if I were playing with an equally expert player I should know that the best I could possibly do (barring my opponent's blunders) would be to secure a draw. As first player, Nought, I should know that I could safely lead with any square on the board. As second player, Cross, I should take a corner if Nought led with a centre and take the centre if he led with anything else. This would avoid many complexities and should always draw. The fact remains that it is a capital little game for children, and even for adults who have never analysed it, but two experts would be merely wasting their time in playing it. To them it is not a game, but a mere puzzle that they have completely solved.

13.   The Horse-shoe Game

Just as in 'Noughts and Crosses', every game should be a draw. Neither player can win except by the bad play of his opponent.

14. Turning the Die

The best call for the first player is either 'two' or 'three', as in either case only one particular throw should defeat him. If he called 'one', the throw of either 3 or 6 should defeat him. If he called 'two', the throw of 5 only should defeat him. If he called 'three', the throw of 4 only should defeat him. If he called 'four', the throw of either 3 or 4 should defeat him. If he called 'five', a throw of either 2 or 3 should defeat him. And if he called 'six', the throw of either 1 or 5 should defeat him. It is impossible to give here a complete analysis of the play, but I will just state that if at any time you score either 5, 6, 9, 10, 14, 15, 18, 19 or 23, with the die any side up, you ought to lose. If you score 7 or 16 with any side up you should win. The chance of winning with the other scores depends on the lie of the die.

15. The Three Dice

Mason's chance of winning was one in six. If Jackson had selected the numbers 8 and 14 his chances would have been exactly the same.

16. The 37 Puzzle Game

The first player (A) can always win, but he must lead with 4. The winning scores to secure during the play are 4, 11, 17, 24, 30, 37. In the first game below the second player (B) puts off defeat as long as possible. In the second game he prevents A scoring 17 or 30, but has to give him 24 and 37. In the third game he prevents A scoring 11 or 24, but has to give him 17, 30 and 37. Notice the important play of the 3 and the 5.

A	B	A	B	A	B
4	1(a)	4	1	4	1
3	1(b)	3	1	3	4
(11)2	1	(11)2	3(d)	(17)5	1
(17)5	1(c)	5	1	3	4
3	2	(24)4	3(e)	(30)5(f)	1
(24)1	2	5	1	3	1
(30)4	1	(37)4		(37)2	
3	2				
(37)1					

(*a*) Or A will score 11 next move. (*b*) B could not prevent A scoring 11 or 17 next move. (*c*) Again, to prevent A immediately scoring 24. (*d*) Preventing A scoring 17, but giving him 24. (*e*) Preventing A scoring 30, but giving him the 37. (*f*) Thus A can always score 24 (as in the last game) or 30 (as in this), either of which commands the winning 37.

17. The Twenty-two Game

Apart from the exhaustion of cards, the winning series is 7, 12, 17, 22. If you can score 17 and leave at least one 5-pair of both kinds (4 – 1, 3 – 2), you must win. If you can score 12 and leave two 5-pairs of both kinds, you must win. If you can score 7 and leave three 5-pairs of both kinds, you must win. Thus, if the first player plays a 3 or 4, you play a 4 or 3, as the case may be, and score 7. Nothing can now prevent the second player from scoring 12, 17 and 22. The lead of 2 can also always be defeated if you reply with a 3 or a 2. Thus, 2 – 3, 2 – 3, 2 – 3, 2 – 3 (20), and, as there is no remaining 2, second player wins. Again, 2 – 3, 1 – 3, 3 – 2, 3 – 2 (19), and second player wins. Again, 2 – 3, 3 – 4 (12), or 2 – 3, 4 – 3 (12), also win for second player. The intricacies of the defence 2 – 2 I leave to the reader. The best second play of first player is a 1.

The first player can always win if he plays 1, and in no other way. Here are specimen games: 1 – 1, 4 – 1, 4 – 1, 4 (16) wins. 1 – 3, 1 – 2, 4 – 1, 4 – 1, 4 (21) wins. 1 – 4, 2 (7) wins. 1 – 2, 4 (7) wins.

18. The Nine Squares Game

I should play M N. My opponent may play H L, and I play C D. (If he had played C D, I should have replied H L, leaving the same position.) The best he can now do is D H (scoring one), but, as he has to play again, I win the remaining eight squares.

19. A Wheel Fallacy

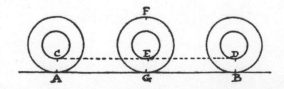

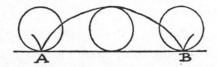

The inner circle has half the diameter of the whole wheel, and therefore has half the circumference. If it merely ran along the imaginary line C D it would require two revolutions: after the first, the point D would be at E. But the point B would be at F, instead of at G, which is absurd. The fact is the inner circle makes only one revolution, but in passing from one position to the other it progresses partly by its own revolution and partly by carriage on the wheel. The point A gets to B entirely by its own revolution, but if you imagine a point at the very centre of the wheel (a point has no dimensions and therefore no circumference), it goes the same distance entirely by what I have called carriage. The curve described by the passage of the point A to B is a common cycloid, but the point C in going to D describes a curtate trochoid.

We have seen that if a bicycle wheel makes one complete revolution, so that the point A touches the ground again at B, the distance A B is the exact length of the circumference, though we cannot, if we are given the length of the diameter, state it in exact figures. Now that point A travels in the direction of the curved line shown in our illustration. This curve is called, as I have said, a 'common cycloid'. Now, if the diameter of the wheel is 28 inches, we can give the exact length of that curve. This is remarkable – that we cannot give exactly the length from A to B in a straight line, but can state exactly the length of the curve. What is that length? I will give the answer at once. The length of the cycloid is exactly four times that of the diameter. Therefore, four times 28 gives us 112 inches as its length. And the area of the space enclosed by the curve and the straight line A B is exactly three times the area of the circle. Therefore, the enclosed space on either side of the circle is equal in area to the circle.

20. A Chain Puzzle

To open a link and join it again will cost 3d. By opening one link at the end of each of the thirteen pieces the cost will be 3s. 3d., so it would be cheaper than that to buy a new chain. If there happened to be a piece of twelve links, all these twelve could be opened to join the remaining twelve pieces at a cost also of 3s. If there had happened to be two pieces together, containing eleven links, all these could be opened to join the remaining eleven pieces at a cost of 2s. 9d. The best that can be done is to open three pieces containing together ten links to join the remaining ten pieces at a cost of 2s. 6d. This is possible if we break up the piece of four links and two pieces of three links. Thus, if we include the piece of three links that was shown in the middle row as one of the three link pieces, we shall get altogether five large links and five small ones. If we had been able to find four pieces containing together nine links we should save another 3d., but this is not possible, nor can we find five pieces containing together eight links, and so on, therefore the correct answer is as stated, 2s. 6d.

21. The Six Pennies

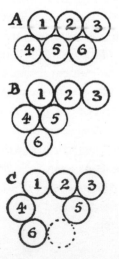

First arrange the pennies as in Diagram A. Then carefully shift 6 and get position B. Next place 5 against 2 and 3 to get the position C. No. 3 can now be placed in the position indicated by the dotted circle.

22. Folding Postage Stamps

Numbering the stamps as in the diagram on p. 85 – that is, 1 2 3 4 in the first row and 5 6 7 8 in the second row, to get the order 1 5 6 4 8 7 3 2 (with No. 1 face upwards, only visible), hold this way, with all faces downwards: $\frac{5678}{1234}$ Fold 7 over 6. Lay 4 flat on 8 and tuck them both in between 7 and 6 so that these four are in the order 7 8 4 6. Now bring 5 and 1 under 6, and it is done. The order 1 3 7 5 6 8 4 2 is more difficult and might well have been overlooked, if one had not been convinced, that according to law, it must be possible. First fold so that 5 6 7 8 only are visible with their faces uppermost. Then fold 5 on 6. Now, between 1 and 5 you have to tuck in 7 and 8, so that 7 lies on the top of 5, and 8 bends round under 6. Then the order will be as required.

23. An Ingenious Match Puzzle

It will be seen that the second I in VII has been moved, so as to form the sign of square root. The square root of 1 is, of course, 1, so that the fractional expression itself represents 1.

24. Fifty-seven to Nothing

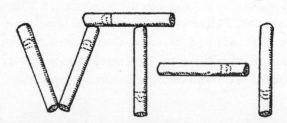

Remove the two cigarettes forming the letter L in the original arrangement, and replace them in the way shown in our illustration. We have the square root of 1 minus 1 (that is 1 less 1), which clearly is 0. In the second case we can remove the same two cigarettes and, by placing one against the V and the other against the second I, form the word NIL, or nothing.

25. The Five Squares

Place the twelve matches as in the diagram and five squares are enclosed. It is true that the one in the centre (indicated by the arrow) is very small, but no conditions were imposed as to dimensions.

26. A Calendar Puzzle

Every year divisible by 4 without remainder is bissextile (leap year), *except* that every year divisible by 100 without remainder is *not* leap year, unless it be also divisible by 400 without remainder, when it *is* leap year. This is not generally understood. Thus 1800 was not a leap year, nor was 1900; but 2000 was a leap year, and 2400, 2800, etc., will all be leap years too. The first day of the last century, 1 January 1901, was *Tuesday*.

Now, the last century contained 25 leap years, because 2000 was a leap year, and therefore 36525 (365×100+25) days, or 5217 weeks and 6 days; so that 1 January 2001, was 6 days later than Tuesday – that is Monday. The present century which began 1 January 2001, will contain only 24 leap years, because 2100 is not a leap year, and 1 January 2101, will be 5 days later than Monday, last mentioned, that is Saturday, because there are 5217 weeks and only 5 days. It will now be convenient to put the results into tabular form, thus:

1	January,	1901 – Tuesday.				
1	"	2001 – Monday.	6	days	later	(2000, leap year)
1	"	2101 – Saturday.	5	"	"	
1	"	2201 – Thursday.	5	"	"	
1	"	2301 – Tuesday.	5	"	"	
1	"	2401 – Monday.	6	"	"	(2400, leap year)

It will thus be seen that the first days of successive centuries will be Tuesday, Monday, Saturday, and Thursday – perpetually recurring – so that the first day of a century can never occur on a Sunday, Wednesday, or a Friday, as I have stated.

27. The Fly's Tour

Before you join the ends give one end of the ribbon a half-turn, so that there is a twist in the ring. Then the fly can walk over all the squares without going over the edge, for we have the curious paradox of a piece of paper with only one side and one edge!

28. A Musical Enigma

The undoubtedly correct solution to this enigma is B A C H. If you turn the cross round, you get successively B flat (treble clef), A (tenor clef), C (alto clef) and B natural (treble clef). In German B flat is called 'B' and B natural 'H,' making it read B A C H.

29. An Arithmetic Puzzle

$6 + \dfrac{6}{6} = 7$.

30. A Digital Puzzle

$22 + 2 = 24$.

31. A Mathematical Puzzle

$3^3 - 3 = 24$.

32.   A Numeral Puzzle

Write nine as IX, take away the I and we have X.

33.   Another Numeral Puzzle

Nine is IX; cross the I and we have XX.

34.   A Numeral Proof

Take the I from XIX and we have XX.

35.   Another Numeral Proof

Write eleven as XI. Then draw a line thus,

$$\frac{\text{VI}}{\text{ΛI}}$$

The upper half is VI.

36.   A Complicated Sum

SIX	IX	XL
IX	X	L
---	---	---
S	I	X

37.   The Fox and the Goose

First he took the goose over, then returned and took the fox over, then brought the goose back and took the corn over, and then returned and took the goose over again.

38.   A Lodging-house Difficulty

The shortest possible way is to move the articles in the following
order: piano, bookcase, wardrobe, piano, cabinet, chest of drawers,
piano, wardrobe, bookcase, cabinet, wardrobe, piano, chest of drawers,
wardrobe, cabinet, bookcase, piano. Thus seventeen removals are
necessary. The landlady could then move chest of drawers, wardrobe,
and cabinet. Mr. Dobson did not mind the wardrobe and chest of
drawers changing rooms so long as he secured the piano.

39.   Minesweeping

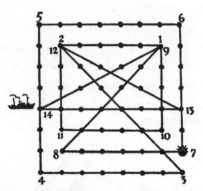

The illustration shows how to pick up the sixty-four mines in fourteen
straight courses under the conditions stated. Go first to 1, then to 2,
then to 3, and so on.

40.   The Cyclist's Journey

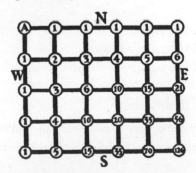

The easiest way to solve this puzzle is to write in the number of routes
to the various towns, as shown in the diagram. After you have written in
1 in all the towns in the top row and the first column, the other
numbers are obtained in this simple way. The number of routes to any
town is the sum of the routes to the two towns immediately above it and
to the left. Then we find that there is only one town that has exactly 21

routes to it, and no more. This is the town that stands close to the letter E. Therefore it is to this town that the cyclist proposed to go.

41. The Rotator Puzzle

Starting from any outside A there are four ways of spelling ATOR; therefore four ways of spelling ROTA, ending with that A. Hence there are sixteen (four times four) ways of spelling ROTATOR with that A in the middle. There are four such outside A's, therefore there are sixty-four (four times sixteen) ways of spelling the word if we use an outside A. Then there are four ways of spelling ATOR from the central A, so that the total involving this A is sixteen. Finally, each of the other four A's gives only two ways of spelling ATOR, and therefore four ways for ROTATOR, or sixteen for all these A's. Add these results together – sixty-four, sixteen and sixteen, and we get ninety-six as the correct answer for all possible ways.

42. The Ten Counters

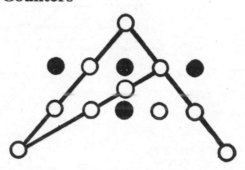

The illustration shows the correct answer. The four shaded counters are the ones that you move to the new positions outside the two lines. They now form five straight rows with four counters in every row.

43. Cryptic Addition

If you turn the page upside down you will find that one, nine, one and eight added together correctly make nineteen.

44. Cupid's Arithmetic

All the young mathematician had to do was to reverse the paper and hold it up to the light, or hold it in front of a mirror, when he would immediately see that his betrothed's curious jumble of figures will read: 'Kiss me, dearest'.

Solutions: Chapter 5.
Word Puzzles

1.   **A Motto Puzzle**

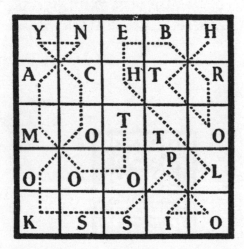

If you start at the central T and follow the dotted line throughout
its route, you will spell out the proberb, 'Too many cooks spoil
the broth'.

2. **Numerical Enigma**

The word is TOBACCO.

3. **Beheadings**

The successive missing words are: eastern, astern, stern, tern, ern, R.N. and N. It is true that the more usual spelling of the sea-eagle is 'erne'.

Note than 'N' also refers to north on a compass.

4. **The Nine-letter Puzzle**

G	E	T
A	I	A
S	U	P

Here is an arrangement that gives as many as thirteen words, if you admit the contraction 'TIS, or twelve without. The words are GET, TEG (a two-year-old sheep), SUP, PUS, PAT, TAP, GAS, SAG, PIG, GIP, SIT, 'TIS, AIA. The last word, AIA, is a Brazilian bird.

5. **Making a Word Square**

L	A	S	H	E	S
A	R	T	E	R	Y
S	T	O	R	M	S
H	E	R	M	I	T
E	R	M	I	N	E
S	Y	S	T	E	M

The first diagram shows the constructed word square, and the lines in the second diagram indicate the pairs of letters that have been exchanged.

6. **A Paradox**

The 'players' were musicians, and as they played music all night they may all very well have 'made quite fair amounts' and lost nothing.

7.   A Palindrome Puzzle

The ten words are Anna, deified, Hannah, madam/minim, noon/naan, otto, peep, reviver and tenet.

8.   Building a Word Square

The letters can be arranged as follows:

P	A	S	T	O	R
A	T	T	I	R	E
S	T	U	P	I	D
T	I	P	T	O	E
O	R	I	O	L	E
R	E	D	E	E	M

9.   A Word Square

T	O	A	S	T
O	T	T	E	R
A	T	O	N	E
S	E	N	S	E
T	R	E	E	S

10.   Natural History

Tompkins's answer was that a horse has four legs, but no horse has five legs; therefore, a horse has fewer legs than no horse.

11.   A Rebus

The words are PAT, TAP and APT.

12.   Missing Words

The following are the five words, all containing the same five letters: PALES, LEAPS, LAPSE, PLEAS and PEALS.

13.   A Buried Quotation

The buried quotation from Shakespeare is, 'The quality of mercy is not strained'.

14. **A Buried Proverb**

The required proverb is, 'A rolling stone gathers no moss.'

15. **Thrice Beheaded**

NASCENT, ASCENT, SCENT, CENT.

16. **A Charade**

TITLE-PAGE.

17. **An Enigma**

The answer is the figure 8.

18. **A Charade**

PRIM-ROSE.

19. **A Charade**

POT-A-TOES.

20. **A Charade**

The required word is PEA-COCK.

21. **A Rebus**

PLUMP, PLUM, LUMP.

22. **A Charade**

The word is NOT-ICE.

23. **An Enigma**

The word is ENGLAND.

24. A Charade

The word is SHOE-STRING.

25. Anagrams

Baker, Auctioneer, Stationer, Tobacconist, Saddler, Sailor, Shoemaker, Lawyers.

26. A Word Square Puzzle

N	E	S	T	L	E	S
E	N	T	R	A	N	T
S	T	R	A	N	G	E
T	R	A	I	T	O	R
L	A	N	T	E	R	N
E	N	G	O	R	G	E
S	T	E	R	N	E	R

27. A Charade

The word is SNOW-DROP.

28. Buried Poets

The eight names are: Gray, Moore, Byron, Pope, Dryden, Gay, Keats and Hemans, in their order.

29. Missing Words

The words are SPRITE, STRIPE, RIPEST and PRIEST, in their order.

30. Missing Words

The words are: DETAINS, STAINED, INSTEAD and SAINTED, which all contain the same letters.

31. Decapitations

The answer is CHAIR, HAIR and AIR.

32.   An Enigma

The king was DAVID.

33.   Anagrams

The twelve rivers are: Rhine, Loire, Tagus, Moselle, Dniester, Tiber, Weser, Rhone, Meuse, Dnieper, Severn and Medway.

34.   A Strange Word

Nowhere – Now here.

35.   A Charade

Ta-lb-ot.

36.   A Charade

Co-nun-drum.

37.   A Cryptic Word

The word is Excommunication. Thus:

| (E) | (10) | (100) | (0) | (1000) | (1000) | (UNI) | (100) | (AT) | (X) | (N) |
| (E) | (X) | (C) | (O) | (M) | (M) | (UNI) | (C) | (AT) | (IO) | (N) |

38.   The Missing Letters

Add the two letters S and Y to each word, and the following new eight words may be formed: YACHTS, TYPES, MISERY, DYERS, STYLE, YEAST, SATYR, PHYSIC.

39.   A Strange Charade

The word is FOUR-SCORE.

40. **Seven Anagrams**

The solutions to the seven anagrams are as follows:

1. William Shakespeare.
2. Oliver Goldsmith.
3. William Hogarth.
4. Joshua Reynolds.
5. James Hogg.
6. John Gay.
7. Wordsworth.

41. **A Clever Anagram**

To make one word out of NEW DOOR we simply rearrange the letters as follows: ONE WORD!

42. **A Sparkling Puzzle**

The Sparkling puzzle is solved in this way: SPARKLING, SPARKING, SPARING, SPRING, SPRIG, PRIG, PIG, PI, I.

43. **A Remarkable Plant**

TOBACCO.

44. **An Elegant Charade**

IN-SAT-IATE. (*In* my first, my second *sat*, my third and fourth *I ate*.)

45. **Word Reversals**

LEVER-REVEL, LEPER-REPEL, DEVIL-LIVED, LIAR-RAIL, MOOD-DOOM.

46. Alphabetical Conundrums

The answers are as follows: A is the middle of DAY. B because it makes OIL BOIL. C because it makes CLASSES of LASSES. D because it is an extremity of LAND. E because it is the end of LIFE. F because it is the capital of FRANCE. G because it makes a LAD GLAD. H because it makes the EAR HEAR. I because it is the centre of BLISS. J because it is close to the eye (I). K because it is the end of PORK. L because it is at the end of the TUNNEL. M because it makes ORE MORE. N because it makes A STY NASTY. O because all the others are in AUDIBLE (inaudible). P because it makes A PA. Q because it is always followed by you (U). R because it is next to Kew (Q). S because it makes HOT SHOT. T because it is in the middle of WATER. U because it is always in TROUBLE and DIFFICULTIES. V because it is always in LOVE. W because it makes ILL WILL. X because it stands for annex (an X). Y because it is in the middle of the EYE. Z because it is to be found in the Zoo.

47. An Arithmetical Charade

CIVIL. Thus: L (50) multiplied by 2 equals C (100). Divide C by 20 and you have V. Divide V by 5 and you have I.

48. Missing Words

CAT, EWE, CUR, RAM. Making EDUCATION, BREWERY, PRECURSOR, PYRAMID.

49. Missing Words

TOPS, POTS, STOP, SPOT, POST.

50. A Charade

SEA-SON-ABLE.

51. Find the Word

The monosyllable is ARE, which, after we have added A, becomes AREA, a word of three syllables.

52. A Conundrum

The answer is that the *road* goes up the hill and down the hill, yet never moves.

53. Missing Words

INLETS-SILENT-LISTEN-ENLIST-TINSEL.

54. An Enigma

The words are NOTE, NOT.

55. An Enigma

The word is O-X-FOR-D. Of course, FOR is three-fifths of FORTY, or 'two score' – that is, three-fifths of the number of the letters in the word.

56. A Charade

The word is MISS-I-ON-ARIES.

57. Beheading

The word is FOX, which becomes OX and X.

58. Five Anagrams

The words are SOVEREIGNTY, CONGRATULATE, DISAPPOINTMENT, MATRIMONY and SWEETHEART.

59. An Enigma

The words are HE, HER, HERO, HEROINE.

60. A Charade

The word is STAG-NATION.

61.   A Transposition

The two words are SPECTRE and RESPECT.

62.   A Charade

The word is CORK-SCREW.

63.   Beheading and Curtailing

The words are: TRUMP, RUMP and RUM.

64.   An Enigma

The word is CAST-A-NET.

65.   An Anagram

The words are SLIP and LIPS.

66.   An Enigma

The two letters are AN, and with the different heads we get BAN, CAN, DAN, FAN, MAN, PAN, RAN, TAN, VAN, WAN.

67.   A Charade

The word is CAR-PET.

68.   A Charade

The word is OFF-ICE.

69.   Curtailment

The words are PLANET, PLANE and PLAN.

70.   An Anagram

HENRY WADSWORTH LONGFELLOW.

71.   **A Numbered Charade**

The word is WELLINGTON.

72.   **An Enigma**

A pair of spectacles.

73.   **An Enigma**

The answer is NOISE.

74.   **A Charade**

The word is NAME-LESS.

75.   **An Anagram**

The word is CHOCOLATE.

76.   **A Charade**

The word is ASS-ASS-I-NATION.

77.   **An Enigma**

A pair of spurs.

78.   **A Transposition**

The words are WRECK and CREW.

79.   **A Charade**

The word is WORM-WOOD.

80.   **An Anagram**

TIME, EMIT, ITEM, MITE.

81. An Enigma

The words are SEVEN, EVEN and EVE.

82. An Anagram

GANDER, DANGER and GARDEN.

83. A Charade

The word is US-HER.

84. A Surprising Relationship

If there are two men, each of whom marries the mother of the other, and there is a son by each marriage, then each of such sons will be at once uncle and nephew of the other. There are other ways in which the relationship may be brought about, but this is by far the simplest.

85. Lost Property

The town was Perth.

86. The City Luncheons

The men may be grouped as follows, where each line represents a day and each column a table.

AB	CD	EF	GH	IJ	KL
AE	DL	GK	FI	CB	HJ
AG	LJ	FH	KC	DE	IB
AF	JB	KI	HD	LG	CE
AK	BE	HC	IL	JF	DG
AH	EG	ID	CJ	BK	LF
AI	GF	CL	DB	EH	JK
AC	FK	DJ	LE	GI	BH
AD	KH	LB	JG	FC	EI
AL	HI	JE	BF	KD	GC
AJ	IC	BG	EK	HL	FD

Note that in every column except the first all the letters descend cyclically in the same order, B, E, G, F, up to J, which is followed by B.

87. The Muddletown Election

The number of votes polled respectively by the Liberal, the Conservative, the Independent, and the Socialist were 1,553, 1,535, 1,407 and 978. All that was necessary was to add the sum of the three majorities 739 to the total poll of 5,473 (making 6,212), and divide by 4, which gives us 1,553 as the poll of the Liberal. Then the polls of the other three candidates can, of course, be found by deducting the successive majorities from the last-mentioned number.

88. That Puzzling Dog

The dog ran on the *other* side of the lady.

89. The Four Cross-roads

All I had to do was to pick up the signpost, hold it over the hole from which it had been taken with the arm bearing the name of the town from which I had come pointing in that direction.

90. Who was First?

Biggs, who saw the smoke, would be first; Carpenter, who saw the bullet strike the water, would be second; and Anderson, who heard the report, would be last of all.

91. Defective Punctuation

Transfer the semicolons to the middle of the lines, and the verses will read as follows:

I saw wood; floating in the air

I saw a skylark; bigger than a bear

I saw an elephant;

and so on to the end.

92. More Punctuation

Punctuate the sentence as follows: If 'is' is not 'is', and 'is not' is 'is', what is it 'is not' is, and what is it 'is' is not, if 'is not' is 'is'?

93. A Cunning Answer

It was Sunday. 'When the day after tomorrow (Tuesday) is yesterday, today (Wednesday) will be as far from Sunday as today (Thursday) was from Sunday when the day before yesterday (Friday) was tomorrow.' From Thursday to Sunday is three days, as is also from Sunday to Wednesday.

94. Freddy's Pudding

The third 'it' refers to the piece last cut off; not to the helping. The words in parenthesis will make all clear. 'His mamma cut off a piece from it; the helping was still too large. When she had cut from it another piece, it (the piece just cut off) was too small. But after mamma had cut off from it (the helping) a third piece, it (the helping) was exactly the size he wanted.'

95. The Banker and the Note

Since the identical forged note can be traced through all the transactions, these are all invalid. Therefore everybody stands in relation to his debtor just where he was before the banker picked up the note, except that the butcher owes, in addition, five pounds to the farmer for the calf received. But if the banker accepts the note from the laundry-woman as if it were good, then destroys it after charging his private account with the amount, everything will be right.

96. Getting the Wine

The man simply pushed the cork in.

97. What are They?

In the lines beginning, 'Twice eight are ten of us, and ten but three,' simply count the letters in the words. Thus, 'eight' contains five letters, and twice five equals ten; 'ten' contains three letters, and so on throughout.

98. Strange, though True

If the horse is put in any mill in which he travels in a circle in a clockwise direction, the near legs pass over more ground than the off legs, since they make a larger circle. This applies not only to Sussex, but to anywhere.

99. A Historical Puzzle

Read the first line of the first verse, then the first line of the second verse, next the second line of the first verse, then the second line of the second verse, and so on, when the treasonable character of the lines will be apparent.

100. Strange Arithmetic

Half of FIVE (that is, of the number of letters in the word) is IV (two letters), and if from this we take one (I), then five (V) remains.

101. Some Maxims

The five maxims are read in this way: First read alternately from the first and second rows, as follows: 'Never tell all you may know, for he who tells everything he knows often tells more than he knows.' Now read the first and third rows in the same way: 'Never attempt all you can do,' etc.; then the first and fourth rows; then the first and fifth; and finally the first and sixth.

102. The Three Tea-cups

Place two lumps in the first cup, one lump in the second cup, and seven lumps in the third cup. Now if you place the second cup in the first cup there is an odd number in every cup, for if a cup contains another cup it also contains the contents of that second cup. There are fifteen different solutions in all.

103. The Handcuffed Spies

The following is a solution. Every spy will be found to have been handcuffed to every other spy once, and only once:

1 2 3	2 6 8	6 1 7	1 4 8	7 2 9	4 3 1
4 5 6	5 9 1	9 4 2	2 5 7	3 6 4	5 8 2
7 8 9	3 7 4	8 3 5	6 9 3	8 1 5	9 7 6

Note that every man is twice in the middle of a triplet, and on four occasions is on the outside. Thus he is handcuffed altogether on eight occasions, or once to each of the other eight men.

104. The Lost Battle

There were 24,000 men in all.

105. A Strange Sentence

Opium and beer, effeminacy and tears, are usually enemies to energy and ought to be odious to you, dear Ellen.

106. Another Strange Sentence

Oh! Emily, benign and effeminate, before you extenuate any excess, use a wise one's assistance.

107. A Riddle

COMIC

108. A Charade

NAPKIN.

109. Another Charade

CHINCHILLA.

110. Enigmatic Names of Birds

a) BIRD OF PARADISE.

b) GULL.

c) ROOK.

d) JAY.

e) WREN.

f) TURKEY.

g) LARK.

h) CRANE.

i) RAIL.

j) QUAIL.

k) SWALLOW.

l) KITE.

111. Enigmatic Names of Beverages

a) PORT.

b) CHAMPAGNE.

c) MADEIRA.

d) SPIRITS.

e) TEA.

112. Enigmatic Names of Plants

a) DANDELION.

b) DAISY.

c) CROW FOOT.

d) MORNING GLORY.

e) YEW.

f) COWSLIP.

113. A Riddle

WALLACE.

114. A Conundrum

HOUR GLASS.

115. A Charade

The letter 'o'.

116. A Charade

PENKNIFE.

117. Beheading and Transposing

The words are FOWL, OWL, WOLF.

118. A Charade

The word is WINDMILL.

119. A Transposition

The words are AMEN, NAME, MEAN, MANE.

120. A Charade

The word is CANDLESTICK.

121. The Traveller's Puzzle

The name of the book is 'ROBINSON CRUSOE.' Start at the upper blank and pass to the letters in this order: R in Sunburn, O and B in Ablution, I and N in Diamonds, first S and O in Obverses, N and C in Neologic, R and U in Upholder, S and second O in Solution, and E and the lower blank in Puzzler. All the letters have been struck out once and once only in the fewest possible straight lines, and the letters at the turnings spell the name of the book.

Solutions: Chapter 6.
Modern Puzzles

1. Battleships

a)

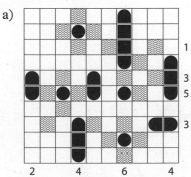

b)

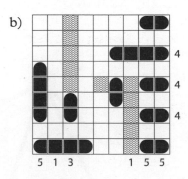

2. Elastic Bands

a)

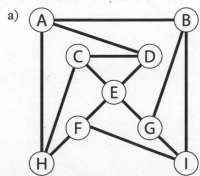

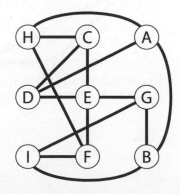

b)

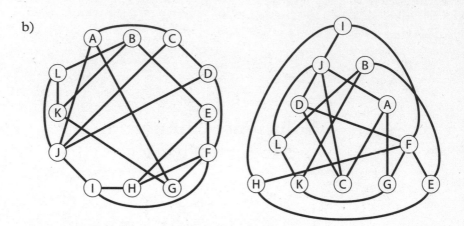

3. Mastermind

a) WARM

b) DREAM

c) STRAND

4. Connections

a)

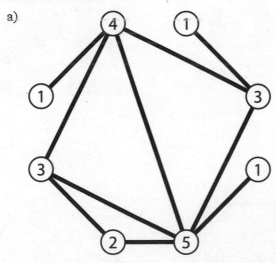

b)

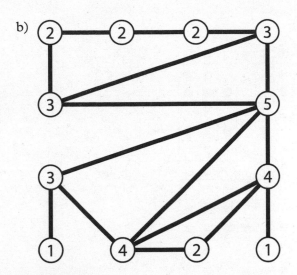

5. Fillomino

a)

	1							
	2		3	3	5	3	2	1
	3							
	4							
	5		5	2		5		
	6		5	5		5		
						4		
						3		
3	1	2	4	10	5	2		
						1		

b)

	2	7	3			5	1	5
	7		2			1		7
	3	2	1			6	5	7
			3	6				
			6	3				
	1	2	4			6	5	2
	6		6			5		5
	4	6	4			5	5	2

6. Minesweeper

a)

●	●		●	●	●	●		●	●
●	5		3	4	4	3		6	●
●	●			●			●	●	●
●	4	●		2	2			5	
	4		2		●	2	●	2	●
●	2	●	2			2		2	
	2		●	2	2			1	
				●		●	●		
	2	●	4	2	4	5	●	6	●
		●		●		●	●	●	●

b)

●	●	●	●	●	●	●		●	2
●	6	5	5	6	6	4	4	●	
●	●		●	●	●	●		4	●
	●	4	3	4	3		●	5	
●	3		●			4	●	4	●
●	4		2		●	●		4	
●	3	●		2	4	4	4	●	●
	4			●		●	●		●
●	●	3	4	3	4	3	3	4	●
2		●	●	●		●			●

7. Graffiti

a)

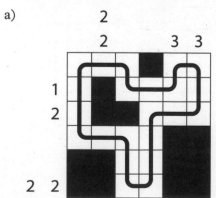

b)

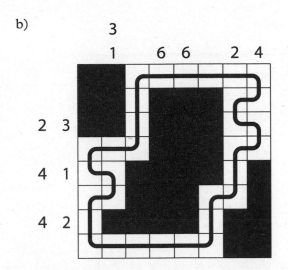

8. Word Search

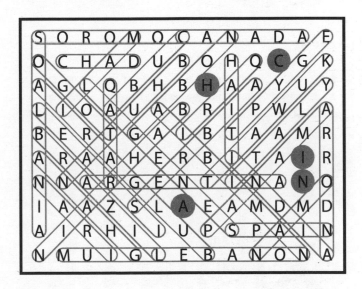

9. Bent Word Search

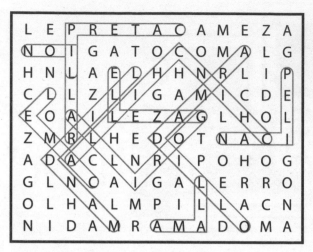

```
L E P R E T A O A M E Z A
N O I G A T O C O M A L G
H N L A E L H H N R L I P
C D L Z L I G A M I C D E
E O A I L E Z A G L H O L
Z M R L H E D O T N A O I
A D A C L N R I P O H O G
G L N O A I G A L E R R O
O L H A L M P I L L A C N
N I D A M R A M A D O M A
```

ALLIGATOR, CROCODILE

10. Word Search

```
B E N E C M C B U M V I S T A M F K O
U S T A O R I E N A J E D O I R H R B
P K L H E G R E K P N B Q K C W S A I
A O R P R O W R F A B S U D F I N L E
C P I V I Y S D T J O T I M O G E J H
H R W A O G N T E N R E N N A B N E A
E I O R N A X H A G A V S L N I C V W
S V K I R A S C A M E O O J J O E I M
T N J C N E B E Y M F R A C S P L C P
L I M D E L K R L I E O N B T A Z A G
B C H K S N O T A N N B R U O T C N A
O A O P O R E U T S G N T D R I I P N
P Y I D D T L S N K O F W A E J L M A
A S N N M U V G A B L V L P I A R Y S
Z O X A O E P I N N O I D E Y D A O T
L O H I Y S H A W A C T B S G M L R A
M E B N O M R N L U B N A T S I J K M
Q U S E I E Z E R V S R I M P L E B A
L D O R P N I G L A X M H K A C D L O
```

11.   Password Path

a)

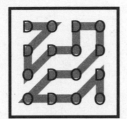

b)

12.   Alphabet Blocks

a)

A	B	C	F
E	D	G	K
M	H	L	O
P	I	N	S
Q	J	T	U
W	R	Y	V

b)

A	B	C	D
F	N	E	G
H	P	I	K
M	V	J	S
O	X	L	T
R	Y	U	Z

13. Build a Criss-cross

a) Category: Capitals

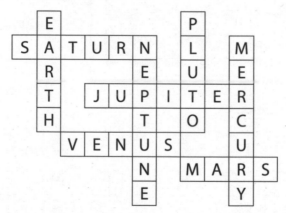

b) Category: In Orbit

14. Mini Quiz

a)

Q1.
How many times
is "A" chosen
in this quiz?

A. 0
B. 1
C. 2

Q2.
How many times
is "B" chosen
in this quiz?

A. 0
B. 2
C. 1

Q3.
How many times
is "C" chosen
in this quiz?

A. 0
B. 1
C. 2

b)

Q1. Answer of Q2 minus answer of Q3 equals	Q2. Answer of Q3 minus answer of Q4 equals	Q3. Answer of Q5 plus answer of Q4 equals	Q4. Product of answers for Q1, Q2 and Q3 is	Q5. Sum of all answers in this quiz equals
A. −1	A. −2	(A.) −1	(A.) −2	A. −1
B. 1	B. −1	B. 1	B. −1	(B.) 1
(C.) 2	(C.) 1	C. 2	C. 1	C. 2

c)

Q1. Are the answers for Q2 and Q3 the same?	Q2. Are the answers for Q1 and Q2 the same?	Q3. Are the answers for Q2 and Q4 the same?	Q4. Are the answers for Q1 and Q2 different?	Q5. Are the answers for Q1 and Q3 the same?
(A.) yes	A. yes	A. yes	(A.) yes	A. yes
B. no	(B.) no	(B.) no	B. no	(B.) no

15. Scrabble

a)

		S	L	O	V	A	K	I	A	
		E						N		
G		R		H			D			
E		B		R	U	S	S	I	A	
R		I		N			A			
M		A		G	U					
A				A	S					
N	E	T	H	E	R	L	A	N	D	S
Y				Y						

b)

		A		B		W		M			
		F	R	E	E	D	O	M		A	N	D
		E				R		A			
J		M				D	U	T	Y		
U		E		S		S		H			S
S		R		I	N			I		G		I
T		C	A	N		H	O	N	O	R		M
I		Y		G		O		G		E		P
C				L		P		S		A	L	L
E	X	P	R	E	S	S	E	D			T	E

16. Count the Shapes

a) 23:

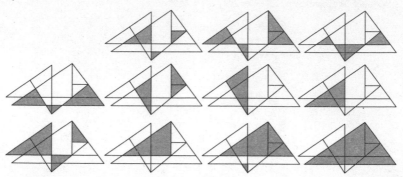

b) 42:

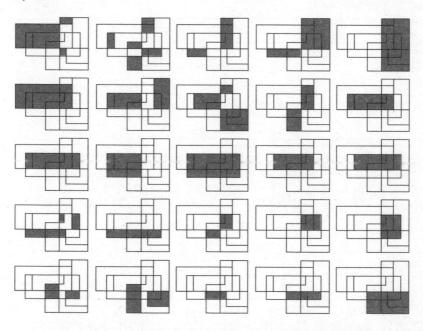

17. Pyramid Climbers

a)

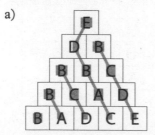

b)

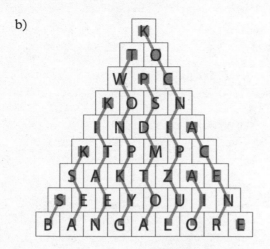

c)

18. Common Letters

a)

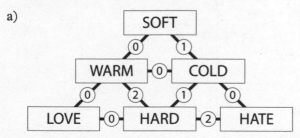

b)

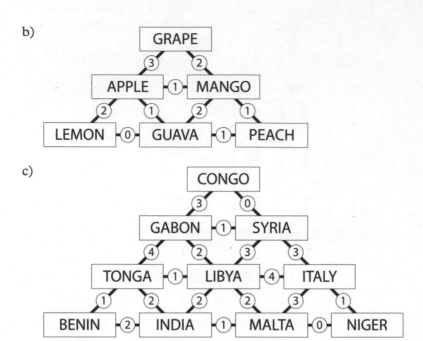

c)

19. Star Gaps

a)

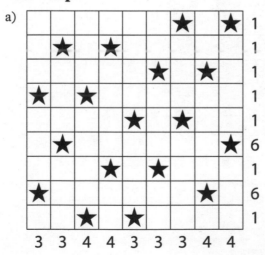

b)

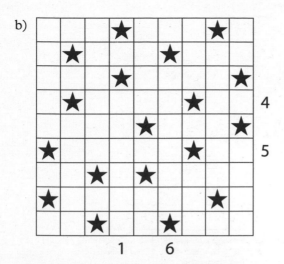

20. Column Dance

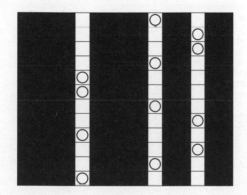

21. Arithmetic Square

a)

$$2 \times 7 - 4 = 10$$
$$\times \quad - \quad +$$
$$9 - 6 - 3 = 0$$
$$- \quad - \quad +$$
$$8 - 1 + 5 = 12$$
$$= \quad = \quad =$$
$$10 \quad 0 \quad 12$$

b)

$$1 \div 3 \times 6 = 2$$
$$\div \quad \times \quad -$$
$$4 \times 2 - 7 = 1$$
$$\times \quad - \quad +$$
$$8 + 5 - 9 = 4$$
$$= \quad = \quad =$$
$$2 \quad 1 \quad 8$$

c)

$$2 \times 8 \times 5 < 83$$
$$+ \quad + \quad +$$
$$3 \times 6 \times 4 < 74$$
$$+ \quad + \quad +$$
$$9 \times 1 \times 7 < 65$$
$$> \quad > \quad >$$
$$13 \quad 14 \quad 15$$

22. Arukone

a)

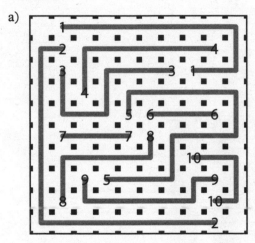

b)

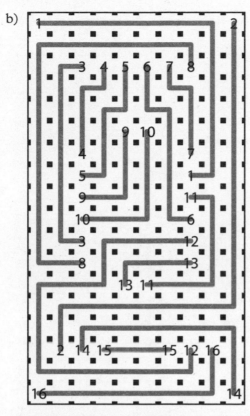

c)

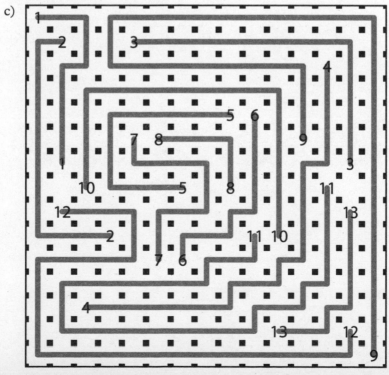

Author Credits

The puzzles in chapters two to five of this book are sourced from the following books:

- *Modern Puzzles* by Henry Dudeney
- *A Puzzle-Mine* by Henry Dudeney
- *Puzzles and Curious Problems* by Henry Dudeney
- *The World's Best Word Puzzles* by Henry Dudeney
- *The Santa Claus' Book of Games and Puzzles* by John H. Tingley
- *Conundrums, Riddles and Puzzles* by Dean Rivers
- *Merry's Book of Puzzles* edited by Robert Merry

The puzzles in chapter six were written by the following authors:

- Silke Berendes
- Andrey Bogdanov
- Branko Ćeranić
- Matus Demiger
- Zoltán Horváth
- Bram de Laat
- Čedomir Milanović
- Prasanna Seshadri
- Thomas Snyder
- Nikola Živanović

Acknowledgements

Many thanks to Zoe Walker for additional puzzle research.

YOUR NOTES